{ *Vintage Collage-Works* }

REPUBLIQUE CENTRAFRICAINE

0ᶠ50

POSTES

CYMOTHOE SANGARIS

VINTAGE

Collage-Works

ARTFUL IDEAS WITH ANTIQUE EPHEMERA

MARYJO & SUNNY KOCH

Produced & Designed by Jennifer Barry

Photographs by Wendy Candelaria

Text by Carolyn Miller

BEVERLY MASSACHUSETTS

QUARRY BOOKS

First published in the United States of America by
Quarry Books, a member of
Quayside Publishing Group
100 Cummings Center, Suite 406-L
Beverly, Massachusetts 01915
Telephone: (978) 282-9590
Fax: (978) 283-2742
www.quarrybooks.com

Library of Congress Cataloging-in-Publication Data

Koch, Maryjo.
Vintage collage-works : artful ideas with antique ephemera / Maryjo &
Sunny Koch ; produced & designed by Jennifer Barry ; photographs by
Wendy Candelaria ; text by Carolyn Miller.
p. cm.
Includes index.
ISBN 1-59253-390-6
1. Collage. I. Koch, Sunny. II. Miller, Carolyn, 1940- III. Title.
TT910.K635 2008
702.81'2--dc22

2007035970
CIP

ISBN-13: 978-1-59253-390-9
ISBN-10: 1-59253-390-6

10 9 8 7 6 5 4 3 2

Produced and designed by Jennifer Barry Design, Fairfax, CA
Layout Production by Kristen Hall
Photographs by Wendy Candelaria
Text by Carolyn Miller

Printed in Singapore

{ *Contents* }

{ *Introduction* }

*C*ollage is an enchanting technique for making art from the beautiful old things around us. Antique stores, flea markets, second-hand shops, and our homes are troves of vintage goods— from postcards, greeting cards, and photographs to letters and scraps of cloth. Vintage Collage-Works *is an inspirational guide to making art from these precious remnants.*

The tools needed can be found in any art or craft store, and the techniques include painting with gouache to highlight and alter the background of your collage; transferring images; pressing and preserving botanicals; and aging and scumbling, which help to emphasize the vintage quality of your materials and to unify the piece as a whole. Each chapter of this book highlights techniques that will allow you to enrich and vary your collages and hopefully inspire you to make your own imaginative and personalized artwork and decorative objects.

A vintage cigar box holds an array of fabric scraps and collectibles for making collages.

Although the word *collage* simply means "gluing" in French (and comes from the word *coller,* "to stick on"), the art form of collage is far richer than the mere definition of the word. Collage is the act of layering and arranging different images and/or materials to make a piece of art. Almost any material that can be affixed to a surface has been used in collage, from the jewels and gold leaf of religious art in Gothic cathedrals to the broken crockery glued onto canvas by modern painters.

Paper has been pasted onto paper to make patterns or illustrations ever since it was invented in China around 200 B.C., but the modern art form of collage was created by Pablo Picasso when he

The Dadaists took collage to the next level: Eliminating the base of the painting altogether, they created entire works of art using only various pieces of paper glued onto a canvas or wood backing. The technique of collage was the natural result of the technological advances that made it easy to reproduce printed matter, from words and photographs to reproductions of paintings and sheet music. Today, the concept of collage is found in almost every art form—from painting, sculpture, and graphic design to poetry, music, and even architecture. In its largest definition, collage is a way of combining different elements to make a work of art that is greater than the sum of its parts.

Almost any material that can be affixed to a surface has been used in collage to make a piece of art.

glued a piece of oilcloth onto a painting in 1912; the oilcloth had a chair-cane design, and he used it to form the seat of a chair in *Still Life with Chair Caning.* In the artistic fervor of turn-of-the-century Paris, Picasso and Georges Braque were in the midst of inventing Cubism. Collage quickly became a Cubist technique for adding visual depth, texture, topicality, and nuances of meaning to art by pasting ephemera such as scraps of newsprint, cigarette wrappers, playing cards, and sheet music onto a painted background.

The square and rectangular shapes of these printed pieces of paper and cloth reinforced the angular shapes of Cubism. Collage was another way of reinventing painting, adding the element of surprise and novelty to a work. But it's hard not to wonder if Picasso and Braque, in their search to make art new, weren't influenced by seeing the "found" collages all around them in Paris: the walls of layer upon layer of posters for events on the sides of buildings—both torn and fading, new and vibrant—that we can still see in Paris today.

The collages shown in this book range from artwork meant to be framed to decorative and useful objects, such as metal tins and paperweights. The first chapter is devoted to collages made from vintage papers, including old letters, envelopes, postcards, maps, and sheet music. Chapter Two is a guide to transforming various containers, from old cigar boxes and matchboxes to jars, bottles, clay pots, and metal tins. The final chapter concerns natural ephemera, including flowers, leaves, rocks, shells, feathers, bark, and seeds. Each chapter explores techniques that can be adapted and built on for your own original collage pieces.

The following pages illustrate collages from the very simple to the artful and complex, and from the classic to the surprisingly inventive. The vintage materials that are the medium of each collage have all the charm of the past: old-fashioned printed matter, lithographs, photographs, and elegant calligraphy that cries out to be preserved and treasured. The inherent beauty of these vintage goods

is emphasized with paint, ink, and pencil, as well as with materials from craft stores—such as ribbons and special trims—that add the final touch to make each collage complete.

Vintage Collage-Works will help you to explore the wealth of vintage materials around you and show you how to transform them into art. The search for these materials will lead you to explore sources of vintage goods in your community or find new ways of honoring the keepsakes you may already own. And this book will give you the information and inspiration you need to create your own unique collages.

{ *Tools & Techniques* }

Tools needed for the collages in Vintage Collage-Works *include paints, pens, and brushes found in most art stores, plus basic tools such as tape, glue, and paste. Some collage projects are more complex, using a scanner and computer software, but many more simply call for collage materials, an adhesive of some sort, and a surface to affix the materials to. Other tools called for in these projects are those you probably already own: scissors, a ruler, and pinking shears. Following is a list of all the tools needed for the collage projects in this book.*

The tools of the collage artist, from circle templates and adhesives to a choice of brushes and cutting implements. One of the more unusual tools that the authors of this book employ is a paper-covered brick to weigh down and press their collages while they dry.

{ *Tools* }

PAINTS, MEDIUMS, & VARNISHES

Watercolors

Gouache paints

Oxgall

Gel medium

Acrylic matte varnish

Acrylic spray coating (fixative)

PENS, PENCILS, & STAMPS

Blender pens, new and old

Calligraphy pen and ink

Micron pen, black (.005)

Colored pencils

Pencil

Rubber stamps and ink pads

BRUSHES

Scumbling brush or filbert
    brush (for scumbling)

Stencil brush (for paste)

Old watercolor brushes,
    small and medium (for gel,
    gouache, and varnish)

Liner brush (for narrow lines)

Watercolor brushes (for
    painting with watercolors)

PAPER & BOARD

Matte board

White construction paper

Cardboard

Mylar

Photo sticker or label papers

Decorative or handmade papers

TAPES, PASTES, & GLUES

Low-tack tape (painter's tape)

Double-stick tape

Yes! paste

Glue stick

PVA (polyvinyl acetate)
    adhesive

Glitter adhesive

CUTTING & MEASURING TOOLS

X-acto knife or Soft Grip
    razor knife

Cutting mat

Pinking shears

Decorative-edged scissors

Wire cutter

Awl

Japanese screw punch

Stamp punch

Small hand saw

Circle template

Metal ruler

MISCELLANEOUS

Photocopier

Digital scanner

Ink-jet printer

Adobe Photoshop software

iTunes software

Black tea bags and mug

Flower press

Palette knife

Paper-covered brick

Heavy book

Photo corners

Needle and thread

Toothpicks

Pins

Screwdriver

Floral wire

Compass

Plastic drafting triangles

Bar of soap

Bone folder

{ *Techniques: Image Transfers* }

Any image that can be photocopied can be transferred onto a smooth surface, making image transfers one of the most creative techniques for collage. All you need is a black-and-white photocopy of your image, low-tack tape (such as Scotch 3M Safe-Release Painter's Masking Tape) to affix it to the surface you wish to transfer the image to, and two blender pens (Chartpak Blender P-O 201 Ad Markers) one new, one older and partially dried out. The clear blending fluid causes the ink from the photocopy to be transferred onto the chosen surface (the photocopy can be used only once). Image transfers work best on smooth surfaces that are not shiny. Make sure to use copyright-free images; your own original artworks and photographs are among your best sources.

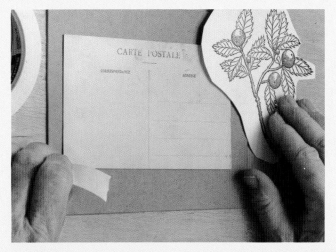

1. Photocopy an image in black and white using a copy machine with a toner cartridge. Tape the copy face down on the surface you're transferring it to.

2. Using a new blender pen, rub over the back of a section of the copy, completely and evenly covering the section.

3. With an older blender pen, repeat the process over the same section using more pressure. Repeat Steps 2 and 3 until the whole image is covered.

4. Lift a corner of the copy to make sure image was thoroughly transferred. If not, repeat Step 2. Discard the copy when finished.

{ *Techniques: Painting with Gouache* }

Gouache is a water-based paint that is rich in pigment, which makes it more opaque and light-reflective than watercolor. Because of its quick application and great coverage, gouache is prized for use in posters and other works of graphic design. Painting with gouache is a quick and effective way to add color to collages, whether you want to highlight some printed element or add new images. All you need is a set of gouache paints and a few inexpensive watercolor brushes (don't use expensive watercolor brushes for gouache). The illustrations that follow will show you, step by step, how to embellish your collage works with butterflies, birds, feathers, and eggs.

BUTTERFLIES

1. Draw in all details first with pencil. Paint in base color.

2. Ink in markings.

3. Paint in brown areas with Van Dyke Brown.

4. Paint in markings with Permanent White. Dry-brush base color over brown areas. Dry-brush Indigo Blue where indicated. Outline with black paint. Shadow with Indigo Blue. Add veins with black paint, then highlight with Permanent White paint. Dry-brush body. Paint in eye with Havannah Lake.

BIRDS

1. Draw in all details and add shading with pencil.

2. Paint head, neck, back, and edges of wing feathers with a mixture of Yellow Ochre, Van Dyke Brown, and olive green. Outline bill and eye with a black Micron (.005) pen. Paint throat and breast with a mixture of Yellow Ochre, Van Dyke Brown, olive green, and a bit of Permanent White. Paint side, abdomen, flank, and undertail Burnt Sienna. Outline feet and all other feathers with black Micron pen.

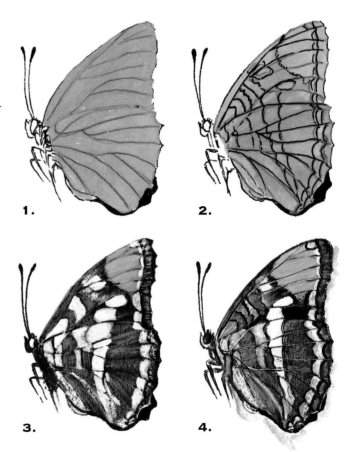

1.

2.

3.

4.

3. Lightly brush a wash of Burnt Sienna on wing feathers. Paint tail feathers and wing feathers Ivory Black. Using a liner brush, outline tail feathers and wing feathers with Permanent White and oxgall. Paint bill Ivory Black.

4. Paint eye with a Van Dyke Brown wash. Using a splayed brush, paint throat and breast with Permanent White mixed with Yellow Ochre. Paint side, abdomen, flank, and undertail with Permanent White mixed with Cadmium Yellow Pale.

5. Brush small area under wing and on top of tail with Van Dyke Brown mixed with a little Permanent White. Shadow underparts with Van Dyke Brown. Using a splayed brush, shadow breast with Van Dyke Brown mixed with black.

6. Using a liner brush, highlight breast with Permanent White mixed with a small amount of Cadmium Yellow.
For eye detail: Paint pupil black. Paint rest of eye with Van Dyke Brown. Shadow top of eye with Van Dyke Brown mixed with a little black. Paint bottom of eye with Permanent White gouache, let dry, and then wash over with Burnt Sienna. Paint eye ring with Van Dyke Brown mixed with a little Permanent White. Highlight center of eye with a dot of Permanent White.
For bill detail: Highlight with Permanent White.
For leg and foot detail: Paint leg and foot Van Dyke Brown. Add black to front edge of leg and foot. Paint claws black. Highlight with Permanent White.

1.   **2.**

3.   **4.**

5.   **6.**

{ *Techniques: Painting with Gouache* }

EGGS

1. Draw the egg outline with a light pencil.

2. Paint in a base coat of Yellow Ochre, Permanent White, and a small amount of Indigo Blue.

3. Use oxgall instead of water to blend in Permanent White over base coat. Highlight with Permanent White: First paint center with thick white, then wash brush, wipe off, and blend to outside edges.

4. Cut a template of the egg out of tracing paper and place it on the egg. Using a stencil brush, splatter in small spots with Burnt Sienna. Remove the template. Using a small, pointed brush, paint in more spots on the edges of the egg.

5. Using the side of a brush, paint in larger spots and scrawls with Burnt Sienna and very light Spectrum Violet. Add darker spots and scrawls with Van Dyke Brown.

6. Create a shadow with Indigo Blue along the edges. When the egg is completely dry, cover it with a Cream 914 Berol pencil, then scrape with an X-acto knife. Shadow the bottom edge with pencil. Highlight the center with dry-brushed Permanent White. Cover the highlight with white pencil; then scrape with an X-acto knife.

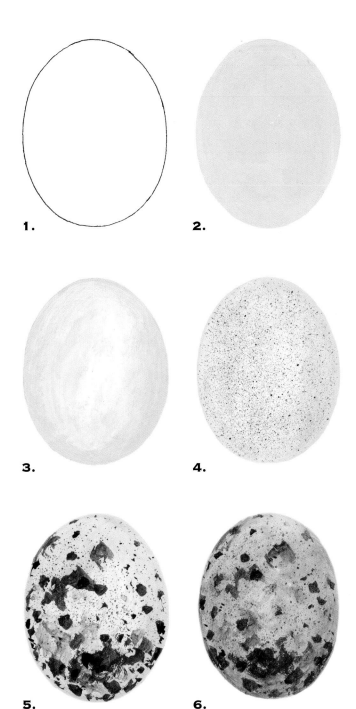

1.   2.

3.   4.

5.   6.

FEATHERS

1. Draw in the feather with a dark pencil (HB). Darken all the bars. Wash over the entire feather with Van Dyke Brown mixed with a little Yellow Ochre and Burnt Sienna.

2. Paint in the bars with Van Dyke Brown mixed with Ivory Black.

3. Wash over the entire feather with Permanent White mixed with very small amounts of Yellow Ochre and Indigo Blue.

4. Wash over the feather with Burnt Sienna and Yellow Ochre in areas of this color. Darken the bars on the left side with a wash of Ivory Black. Darken the bars on the right side with Van Dyke Brown. Wash more Van Dyke Brown toward the quill. Wash over the left side with Van Dyke Brown. Wash over the entire feather with watered-down Permanent White and Yellow Ochre.

5. To paint the quill: Wash Van Dyke Brown down three-fourths of the quill. Line the edges with Ivory Black. Add Permanent White for reflections. For the bottom of the quill, wash with Permanent White mixed with a very small amount of Indigo Blue and Yellow Ochre for a transparent look. Paint heavier Permanent White gouache along the bottom edge of the quill. Paint a little Yellow Ochre or Cadmium Yellow Pale along the top edge. Highlight with Permanent White.

1.

2.

3.

4.

5.

{ *Techniques: Aging & Scumbling* }

Aging techniques give new paper a vintage look so that it can be collaged with vintage documents. The simplest way is to coat the new paper with a thin wash or mottling of brown watercolor. Or you can age paper by tea staining—immersing it in a bath of tea to simulate the look of paper aged naturally. Another technique is to scumble paint over the surface of the collage, giving it a mottled, aged effect. If you haven't tried these techniques before, experiment with extra swatches of your papers to be aged or copies of your artwork that you plan to scumble, following the techniques described below, before starting your collage.

AGING BY TEA STAINING

To age papers by tea staining, simply immerse the paper in brewed tea for several minutes until it reaches the desired aged color; then remove it and allow it to dry. Take care when using delicate paper; tea staining is easier when the paper is fairly heavy.

MATERIALS

Mug, bowl, or tray (depending on the size of paper to stain), black tea bags (one for a mug, several for a bowl or tray, depending on size), tweezers or tongs, paper or cloth towels for drying, electric iron

PROCESS

1. Using a mug, bowl, or tray and black tea bags, brew tea to a medium to dark color. Leaving tea bag(s) in the container, add the paper to be stained. Tea can be warm when adding paper.

2. Checking often (use long-handled tweezers or tongs to lift paper from tea) let paper soak until it reaches the desired color. Be careful with delicate papers; sturdy papers and tags are easier to stain.

3. When paper is the shade you prefer, remove it from tea and let dry on paper or old cloth towels. You may need to change towels to facilitate drying. If the dried paper is excessively wrinkled, iron it carefully on a low setting.

SCUMBLING

Scumbling is the technique of softening the color or outline of a painted image by lightly applying a thin coat of a lighter color of paint with an almost-dry brush. This technique adds an overall layer of color to a collage while letting the ground of the paper show through and giving it an aged appearance at the same time. The surface then looks a little like that of an old painted plaster wall. A layer of scumbled gouache followed by tints of watercolor adds texture.

MATERIALS

Permanent White gouache, Brilliant Gold gouache (optional), set of watercolors, watercolor brushes, Simply Simmons scumbling brush or Royal Softgrip filbert brush (has orange or fuchsia on the tip of the handle)

1. Using Permanent White gouache and scumbling or filbert brush, dry-brush image and any area you want to texture. Let dry.

2. Using a watercolor brush with very little water, apply watercolors to subtlely stain the image, retaining the textured surface of the white paint.

3. Continue adding watercolors until you are pleased with the overall scumbling effect. Let dry.

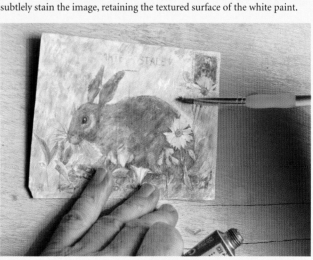

4. If desired, add gold accents and flecks with a filbert brush using gold gouache. Let dry.

{ Techniques: Pressing & Preserving }

Dried botanicals—including flowers, leaves, and seaweed—are exquisite materials for collage; if pressed and preserved correctly, they will last indefinitely and retain much of their color, especially if framed under glass or acrylic. Using botanicals adds intricacy, beauty, and uniqueness to an artwork. And this technique also allows you to preserve natural materials that are especially beautiful or meaningful to you by incorporating them into a collage.

Make sure to let botanicals dry naturally if they are damp. A flower press is ideal for pressing and drying, though you may substitute a large phone book or a stack of heavy books. After they are thoroughly dried in the flower press, they may be preserved by coating them with acrylic matte varnish and allowing them to dry again. After you've affixed the botanicals to your collage, make sure to keep the piece out of the sun or strong light, as the delicate flowers or leaves can fade.

PRESSING BOTANICALS

1. Collect flowers, leaves, seaweed, and other botanicals. If they are damp with moisture, set aside to let surfaces dry before pressing.

2. Use a flower press (or phone book or stack of heavy books) with two pieces of matte board (about ⅛-inch thick) and white construction paper (cut to fit) for every pressing. Don't use corrugated (ribbed) cardboard in place of matte board, or you will have line marks on your pressings.

3. Place a piece of matte board on the bottom of the press and a piece of white construction paper on top of the matte board. Place botanical on the paper. Top it with another piece of construction paper, and then a piece of matte board.

4. Close the press and leave for 24 hours. If the botanical is not dry, change the papers if they are saturated and press again until botanical is thoroughly dried.

5. Using an old watercolor brush, coat the pressed and dried botanical with acrylic matte varnish to protect it. Never place pressed or dried botanicals in the sun, even if they are coated with varnish.

8822
Moth Atlas Atlas

COLLAGE WITH

{ *Vintage Papers* }

Vintage papers to use in collage range from old letters and envelopes to bits of old wallpaper. Old postcards, sheet music, and maps are other charming sources of material for collage. Age often gives paper an appealing golden hue, and some papers are torn or otherwise distressed by time and use. Often the paper itself has a texture and weight that is aesthetically pleasing, while the images and words have an old-fashioned gracefulness. Making collages with antique documents is a way of layering and arranging tokens of the past to create a new work of art.

☞ BIRD SOUL COLLAGE

An old envelope and photograph layered on handmade paper are adorned with a collaged poem; a bird theme is carried out by a feather and bits of eggshell.

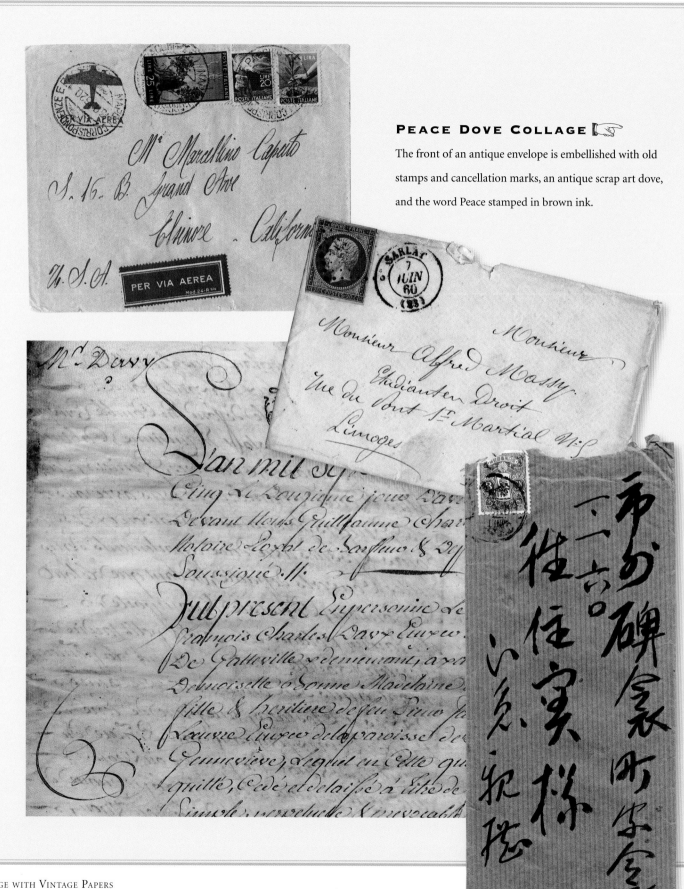

PEACE DOVE COLLAGE ☞

The front of an antique envelope is embellished with old
stamps and cancellation marks, an antique scrap art dove,
and the word Peace stamped in brown ink.

*O*ften beautifully inscribed, old letters and envelopes—from flea markets or your personal archives—have a nostalgic appeal. The paper itself is often of high quality, either tissue-thin or heavy cotton bond, and the unevenness of the ink on the paper and the fineness of the old-fashioned penmanship adds to the charm. Either the front or back of envelopes can be used; both envelopes and sheets of paper can form the background of a collage, or they can be torn or cut to paste onto a background.

PAINTED MOTH ENVELOPE

This antique envelope is the base artwork for legs cut from a *commedia dell'arte* card; a gorgeous painted moth repeats the bronze and gold colors of the art.

PAINTED LETTER & ENVELOPE COLLAGE

An antique French letter and envelope adorned with moths painted in gouache are first pasted onto handmade deckled paper, then onto Italian marbled paper to make a unique collage suitable for framing.

☞ ANTIQUE LETTERS & TRANSFERS FOR STATIONERY LABELS

Labels for files, document boxes, and other items were made from photocopies of reproduced Victorian labels transferred onto pieces of old letters.

MATERIALS

Dover clip art book *(Florid Victorian Ornament)*, copy machine, one new and one old Chartpak Blender P-O 201 Ad Marker, piece of an antique French letter, gouache or watercolor brush, digital scanner, ink-jet printer, 8½- x 11-inch glossy photo sticker paper (Avery brand), X-acto knife, metal ruler, and cutting mat

PROCESS

1. Photocopy ornamental label from Dover book.

2. Using blender pens, transfer the label onto the piece of an antique letter.

3. Using gouache, mix paint colors to match the background of the letter, and paint out the handwriting inside the label. Let dry.

4. Scan the label, add a typeset name inside the ornamental frame, and print it on photo sticker paper using an ink-jet printer. (Follow the instructions, or use an existing label template included with the photo sticker paper.) Cut out the labels using an X-acto knife and ruler, and paste them on stationery.

BIRD & FRENCH POSTCARD COLLAGE

MATERIALS

French postcard, piece of old French envelope with wax seal, Yes! paste, stencil brush for paste, Permanent White gouache, scumbling or filbert brush, watercolors and watercolor brushes, gouache paints, Krylon No. 1303 Crystal Clear acrylic spray coating (fixative), antique bird scrap art

PROCESS

1. Paste a piece of the French envelope scrap to the left side of the postcard.

2. Scumble Permanent White gouache over the entire card.

3. Apply watercolors over scumbling.

4. Using paste, affix the bird to the card.

5. Spray the entire card with Krylon fixative.

*V*intage postcards, with their colorful graphics, make vivid backdrops for collage. Foreign cards—such as those from France, Morocco, and Italy—are especially evocative. The original postage stamps, cancellation marks, addresses, and handwritten messages all add visual interest. Use both the fronts and backs of postcards. Personalize vintage cards to send to friends by pasting over the address and message, or look for cards that have never been written on.

PERSIAN GATE NOTE CARD

The image of an elaborate iron gate was transferred onto an antique postcard. Gouache was scumbled over the images to age and color the card and a Persian postage stamp added to finish the collage. The postcard was then mounted onto a note card with gold photo corners.

PROCESS

1. Photocopy the iron gate image from the Dover book. Using the blender pens, transfer the gate image onto the antique postcard.

2. Scumble Permanent White gouache lightly over the postcard from the left side of the gate to the edge of the card, more heavily over the rock wall of the gate. Paint with watercolors.

3. Using Yes! paste, affix an antique Persian postage stamp.

4. Spray with Krylon fixative.

5. Photocopy the artwork; trim and adhere to the front of a note card with paper photo corners.

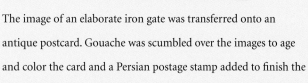

TURBANED MAN POSTCARD

This antique Egyptian postcard with pyramids in the background is the base for a colorful collage using the same techniques of image transfer (of a turbaned man) and scumbling to create a colorful collage. A postage stamp and rubber-stamped words and cancellation marks were added as well.

MATERIALS

Antique postcards, note card for mounting postcard, Dover book (for the gate: *Historic Ornament: A Pictorial Archive*), copy machine with toner cartridge, one new and one old Transfer Chartpak Blender P-O 201 pen, Dover book (for the man *Men: A Pictorial Archive from Nineteenth-Century Sources*), antique postage stamps, rubber cancellation stamps, rubber alphabet stamps, Permanent White gouache, scumbling or filbert brush, watercolors and watercolor brushes, Yes! paste, stencil brush for paste, Krylon No. 1303 Crystal Clear acrylic spray coating (fixative), paper photo corners

PROCESS

1. Photocopy a turbaned man image from the Dover book; using transfer markers, transfer the image onto the postcard.

2. Using Yes! paste, affix an antique Egyptian stamp.

3. Using rubber stamps, add words and cancellation marks.

4. Spray with Krylon fixative.

☞ PHOTOGRAPHIC POSTCARDS ☜

The postcard collages on these two pages were made by pasting antique scrap art or art cut from advertising trading cards onto vintage photographic postcards, then layering the cards with postage stamps, scraps of old letters, and marbleized paper; paint scumbled over the cards adds color and an aged effect.

MATERIALS

Vintage postcards, scraps of antique letters, scissors, antique French trading cards, scrap art of antique birds and flowers, postage stamps, paper-covered brick, Permanent White gouache, scumbling or filbert brush, watercolors and watercolor brushes, Yes! paste, stencil brush for paste, Krylon No. 1303 Crystal Clear acrylic spray coating (fixative)

Process

1. Using paste, affix scraps of antique letters to a postcard.

2. Scumble with Permanent White gouache; then paint with watercolors.

3. Cut out scrap art and affix it to the card with paste.

4. Paste on stamps.

5. Weigh the card down with the covered brick until dry.

6. Spray with fixative.

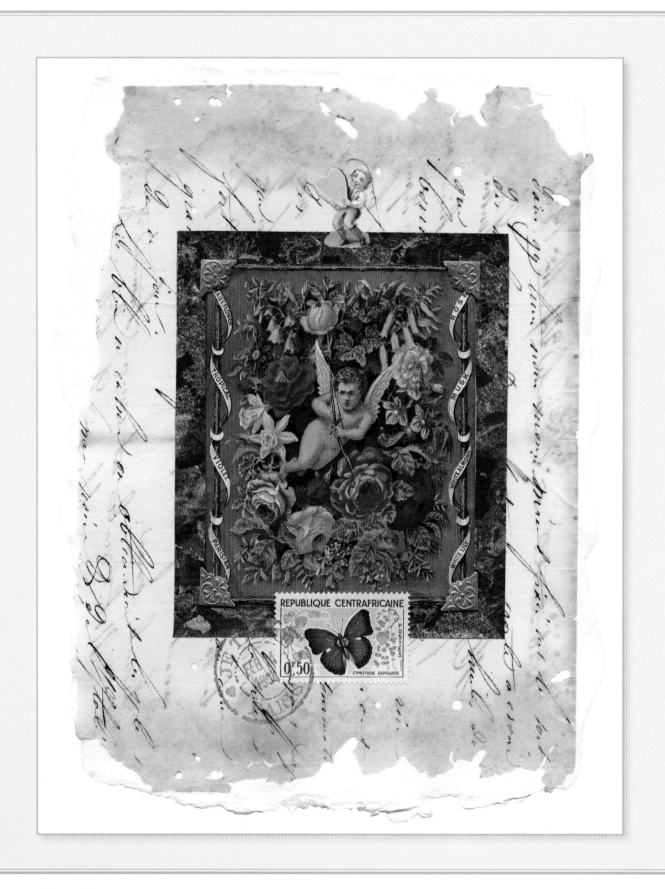

{ *Scrap Art* }

Scrap art images are the easiest way to add color and interesting visuals to collages. There is a vast selection of both antique and reproduced scrap art available for use in scrapbooks. You can find this type of scrap art in almost any theme imaginable; it is widely available at vintage paper fairs and on the Internet. A combination of scrap art, original antique documents, and hand-painted accents make for a memorable and multifaceted collage.

 VICTORIAN VALENTINE COLLAGE

This hand-crafted Valentine combines an antique French letter pasted onto handmade paper, Italian marbled paper, a vintage Valentine, and scrap art; the card is embellished with gold photo corners, rubber stamps, and a foreign postage stamp.

 VICTORIAN SCRAP ART COLLAGE

Scrap art of a Victorian woman in a red-plumed hat was pasted onto an antique postcard along with other ephemera; the finished collage was then color-copied, trimmed, and mounted onto a store-bought note card with gold photo corners.

Scrap Art File Folder

A one-of-a-kind folder for precious documents was made by layering tissue paper, wallpaper, and a torn letter and envelope on a blank file folder; a gold Dresden feather holds the decorative ribbon in place.

Materials

Blank file folder, brown tissue paper, antique wallpaper, antique French letters (torn), antique French envelope, ribbon, gold Dresden feather, Brilliant Gold gouache, old watercolor brush for gouache, Yes! paste, stencil brush for paste, gel medium, old watercolor brush for gel, paper-covered brick

Process

1. Using paste, affix the tissue on the entire folder; add a small strip to inside of top front.

2. Paint edges with gold gouache.

3. Paste on the wallpaper, then the torn letter, then the envelope. Weigh down with the brick until dried.

4. Paste the antique letter to the inside of the folder so that just a little shows; weigh down with the brick to dry.

5. Coat the entire front and back of the file with gel medium.

6. Tie a ribbon around the top of the file, then paste it to the back of the file.

7. Coat the bottom two-thirds of the underside of the Dresden feather with paste, leaving the top unpasted; hook the end of the feather over the front ribbon to hold the ribbon in place.

Pansies & Butterfly Collage

An antique letter is the background for pansy scrap art, postage stamps, and a beautifully hand-painted butterfly.

Materials

Antique French letter, antique postage stamps, pansy scrap art, Permanent White gouache, watercolors and watercolor brushes, Yes! paste, stencil brush for paste, Krylon No. 1303 Crystal Clear acrylic spray coating (fixative)

Process

1. Using Permanent White gouache, paint a butterfly shape on the letter to cover the words completely; paint in the rest of butterfly with gouache paints. (See painting technique for butterflies on page 16.)

2. Using paste, affix stamps.

3. Paste on the pansy scrap art.

4. Spray with Krylon fixative.

BIRD SCRAP ART NOTE CARDS

These exquisite note cards were made by pasting vintage bird trading cards onto handmade leaf paper. If you want to make multiple copies of each card, scan or copy the trading cards and print multiples with a color inkjet printer or color copier.

MATERIALS

Vintage bird trading cards, handmade leaf paper, card stock (5½ x 8½ inches, scored in center), envelopes (size A-2), Yes! paste, stencil brush for paste, paper-covered brick

PROCESS

1. Tear the leaf paper to create a soft edge.

2. Using paste, affix the leaf paper to the front of the card.

3. Paste on either an original bird trading card or a printed copy to the leaf paper. Weigh down with the brick until dry.

☞ SCRAP ART GIFT TAGS

To make these gift tags, antique trading cards were scanned and printed to make multiple copies, then pasted onto office supply tags and tied with a decorative ribbon.

MATERIALS

Scanned and printed copies of antique advertising trading cards, office supply tags, Italian silk ribbon, Yes! paste, stencil brush for paste, scanner and color printer, X-acto knife, metal ruler, cutting mat, paper-covered brick

PROCESS

1. Cut out the individual cards with an X-acto knife and a metal ruler on a cutting mat.

2. Using paste, affix a card to an office supply tag. Weigh down with the brick until dry.

3. Tie on a ribbon.

SCRAP ART & FABRIC NOTE CARDS

Fabric-mounted paper, scrap art, and trading cards were collaged onto heavy card stock to make these flowery note cards. Cutting out the scrap art with decorative-edged scissors or carefully tearing the edges adds an additional vintage look to the collage.

MATERIALS

Fabric-mounted flower paper, scrap art of shoe and flower, trading cards, antique wallpaper trim, gold photo corners, Yes! paste, stencil brush for paste, card stock (7 x 10 inches, scored in center), envelopes, paper-covered brick

PROCESS

1. To affix the fabric-mounted paper directly onto the card stock, brush on the paste to the back side of the paper. Weigh down with the brick until dry.

2. If mounting the collage with photo corners, paste the fabric-mounted paper to a piece of wallpaper trim cut to size.

3. Paste the scrap art (Easter trading card and letter E, cut-out shoe and flower, or fairy) onto the fabric. Weigh down with the brick until dry. Mount the collage to the card stock with photo corners if desired.

Note: To detach a piece of scrap art that is already affixed to an object, such as an old scrapbook, place a damp towel on top of the scrap until it loosens. Run a palette knife gently under the scrap art, lift, and separate it from the paper; set aside, bottom side up, on a sheet of white paper to dry.

☞ SCRAP ART PLACE CARDS

Here, scrap art and scalloped cards were combined to make place cards for guests: The edges of the cards were bordered with gold gouache, and a strip of paper was affixed to each card for inscribing the guest's name with a calligraphy pen.

MATERIALS

Antique trading cards with hands holding flowers, antique bird scrap art, scallop-edged blank cards (3 1/2 x 1 3/4 inches), small strips of paper, Brilliant Gold gouache, watercolor brush for gouache, scissors, X-acto knife, cutting mat, Yes! paste, stencil brush for paste, paper-covered brick, calligraphy pen and ink

PROCESS

1. For the place card with the hand, use an X-acto knife and scissors to cut out the hand with flowers from the antique trading card.

2. Using paste, affix the hand and flowers to the scallop-edged card; repeat if using the bird scrap art.

3. Paint the edges of the small strips of paper with gold gouache; insert into fingers of hands or bills of birds. Weigh down with the brick until dry.

4. Paint the scalloped edges of the cards with gold gouache.

5. Write guests' names on the place cards with pen and ink; put a card at each guest's place.

SCRAP ART BOOKPLATES 👉

Make bookplates for yourself and to give as gifts by collaging antique trading cards onto Italian marbled paper; brush on gold gouache to gild the edges.

MATERIALS

Italian marbled paper, antique trading cards with images of artists' palettes or flowers, calligraphy pen and ink, Yes! paste, stencil brush for paste, paper-covered brick, Brilliant Gold gouache, watercolor brush for gouache, scissors, X-acto knife, cutting mat

PROCESS

1. Cut the marbled paper ⅜ inch larger on all sides than the trading cards.

2. Paint the edges of each trading card with the gold gouache.

3. Using paste, affix each card to a piece of marbled paper. Weigh down with the brick until dry.

4. Using the pen and ink, write "This book belongs to" on each card.

5. Paste the bookplates into books, or make several to give as a gift.

{ *Wallpaper* }

Old rolls of wallpaper can be hard to find, but are available at some antique stores and flea markets. The Victorian era produced a wealth of patterned wallpaper, some of it hand-printed using wood blocks. Look for old wallpaper sample booklets and sample rolls, as well as rolls of wallpaper border trim. A scrap of old wallpaper or wallpaper trim adds another intriguing layer of color, pattern, and texture to a collage—or it can be a theme in itself.

☞ Antique wallpaper is the dominant material in this unique collage created by assembling multiple layers of wallpaper scraps, a girl's photograph, and other unusual ephemera.

👉 ANTIQUE WALLPAPER & POSTCARD COLLAGE

A scrap of French floral wallpaper was pasted onto an old foreign postcard to make this collage; a yellow butterfly, painted by hand, complements the flowers.

MATERIALS

Antique postcard, antique French floral wallpaper, Permanent White gouache, watercolors and watercolor brushes, Yes! paste, stencil brush for paste, paper-covered brick, Krylon No. 1303 Crystal Clear acrylic spray coating (fixative)

PROCESS

1. Paste the floral wallpaper onto the postcard. Weigh down with the brick until dry.

2. Paint the butterfly by using Permanent White gouache first, and then applying watercolors. *(See painting technique for butterflies on page 16.)*

3. Spray with fixative.

Antique Wallpaper Mini-Journals

Perfect for gift-giving, these artful little journals were made by covering blank booklets with wallpaper trim. The butterfly wallpaper journal features an old button and a ribbon as a clever closure. The floral wall-paper on the other journal was scumbled with gouache; then scrap art and a wax seal were added to complete the collage.

Materials

Small blank booklet (3 x 5 inches), wallpaper trim, decorative paper for inside covers, ribbon, button, Yes! paste, stencil brush for paste, awl, needle, paper-covered brick, X-acto knife, metal ruler, cutting mat, antique scrap art bird, sealing wax and seal, lighter or match, Permanent White gouache, scumbling or filbert brush, gel medium, Brilliant Gold gouache

Process

1. Measure and cut the wallpaper to fit the front and back of the booklet.

2. Using a stencil brush, spread paste on the front of the booklet.

3. Place the wallpaper on the front cover and weigh down with the brick until dry. Repeat Steps 2 and 3 for the back cover.

4. Measure and cut the decorative paper to fit the inside covers.

5. For a button and ribbon closure, hold the button in place on the cover and mark the buttonholes with a pencil. Remove the button and make the holes with an awl. Using a needle, pull the ribbon through the buttonholes. Tie the ribbon in a bow.

6. Paste the paper on the inside covers as in Steps 2 and 3. Weigh down with the brick until dry.

7. For the scrap art and scumbled journal, scumble gouache over the wallpaper and booklet spine on the front and back and let dry.

8. Paste on the scrap art bird and the piece of scrap card. Weigh down with the brick until dry.

9. Melt the sealing wax to drip in the center of the scrap card; press with a seal.

10. Brush some gold gouache onto the wax seal.

11. Coat the front with gel medium and let dry; repeat on the back.

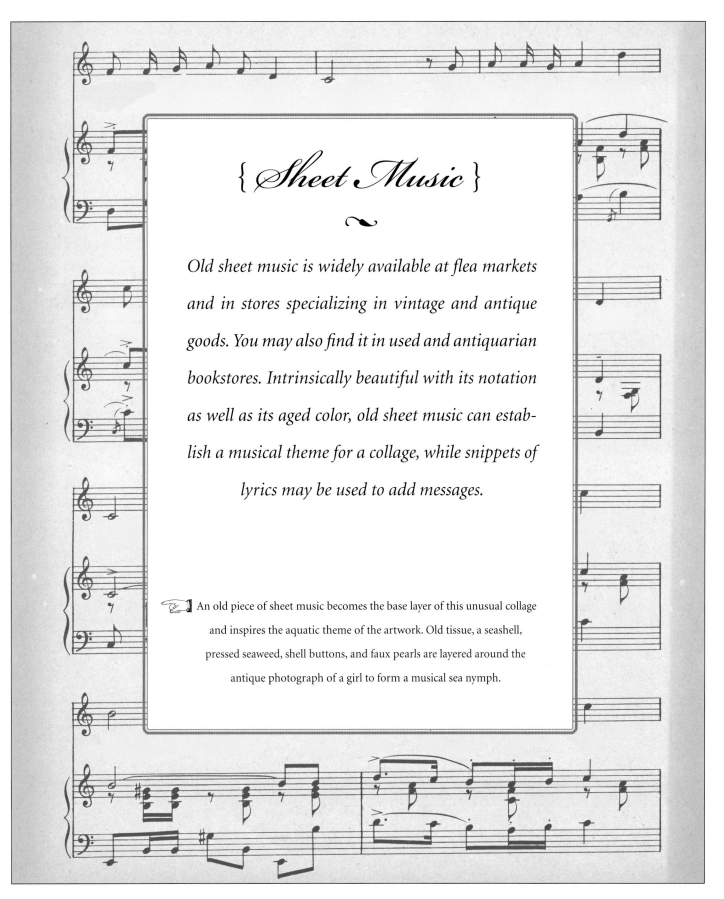

{ *Sheet Music* }

Old sheet music is widely available at flea markets and in stores specializing in vintage and antique goods. You may also find it in used and antiquarian bookstores. Intrinsically beautiful with its notation as well as its aged color, old sheet music can establish a musical theme for a collage, while snippets of lyrics may be used to add messages.

An old piece of sheet music becomes the base layer of this unusual collage and inspires the aquatic theme of the artwork. Old tissue, a seashell, pressed seaweed, shell buttons, and faux pearls are layered around the antique photograph of a girl to form a musical sea nymph.

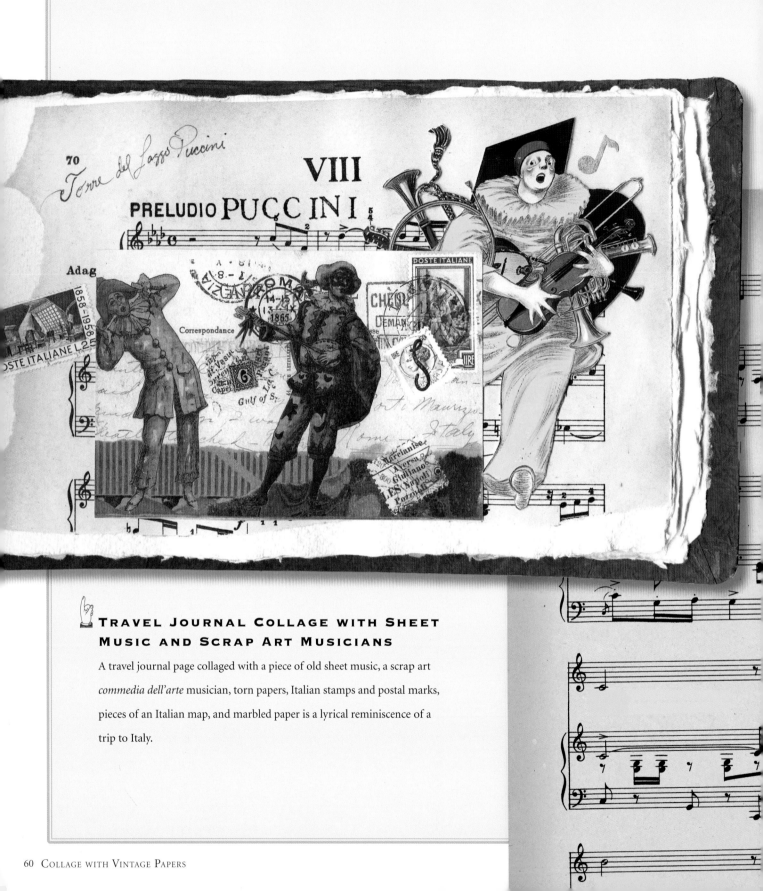

☞ TRAVEL JOURNAL COLLAGE WITH SHEET MUSIC AND SCRAP ART MUSICIANS

A travel journal page collaged with a piece of old sheet music, a scrap art *commedia dell'arte* musician, torn papers, Italian stamps and postal marks, pieces of an Italian map, and marbled paper is a lyrical reminiscence of a trip to Italy.

KEEPSAKE TIN COLLAGE WITH SHEET MUSIC

A piece of sheet music and an antique scrap art bird grace the metal-papered top of this tin; natural fiber trims the outer edge of the lid.

MATERIALS

Round metal tin, antique scrap art bird, antique scrap sheet music, scrap metal paper (self-adhesive, from Mrs. Grossman's), natural fiber, felt, Yes! paste, stencil brush for paste, scissors, paper-covered brick

PROCESS

1. Measure and cut the scrap metal paper to fit the tin top and sides. Apply to the tin top.

2. Using paste, affix the music scrap and the scrap art bird.

3. Paste strips of fiber around the outer edge of lid.

4. Measure and cut the felt to fit the bottom of the tin. Paste on the felt and weigh down with the brick until dry.

SHEET MUSIC COLLAGES FOR CD JEWEL CASE INSERTS AND DISC LABELS

A personalized CD makes a priceless gift, from the unique playlist and CD label to the one-of-a kind jewel case cover collaged with sheet music, decorative papers, gold Dresden owl, and black Dresden trim.

i wish you love

Sea Songs

CD Labels

One-of-a-kind CD labels can be created using Adobe Photoshop computer software and inkjet CD label paper. You can scan artwork with Photoshop, add type and colors, and print your own CD labels using the CD label software that comes with the adhesive pre-cut label sheets.

i wish you love

1. I Wish You Love / Rosemary Clooney
2. You Love Me / DeVotchKa
3. Words / Shawn Colvin
4. This Never Happened Before / Paul McCartney
5. Let It Be Me / Rosie Thomas
6. Mona Lisa / Grant Lee Phillips
7. Walk Away Renee / Linda Ronstadt & Ann Savoy
8. The Grass Is Blue / Norah Jones
9. Meet Me by the Water / Rachael Yamagata
10. Gold In the Air of Summer / Kings of Convenience
11. Fields Of Gold / Sting
12. The Beauty of the Rain / Dar Williams
13. Hope On Board / Tom Petty

Materials

Dover book (*Animals*), blank CD, CD jewel case, Avery Matte White CD/DVD Labeling System for ink-jet printer (includes labels, applicator, and application software), sheet music, decorative papers, colored ink-jet paper/stationery, gold Dresden owl, black Dresden trim, self-adhesive gold photo corners, Adobe Photoshop software, iTunes software, inkjet printer, scanner, Yes! paste, stencil brush for paste, glue stick, X-acto knife, metal ruler, cutting mat

Process for CD Labels

1. Scan the clip art image of the owls from the Dover book and combine with a color background layer using Photoshop.

2. Open the CD-label software (Avery DesignPro, media edition); click on "Design from Scratch" and select template no. 8931.

3. Insert the clip art file and fit it onto the template.

4. For the title of CD, insert circular text and fit onto the template.

5. Print the label and affix it to a burned CD with the applicator.

PROCESS FOR CD JEWEL CASE INSERT:

1. Select the music playlist using your favorite CD burning software.

2. Burn the music playlist onto a blank disc.

3. To print the playlist on colored paper, go to the "File" menu in iTunes, select "Print", then select "Jewel Case Insert", then "Theme: Text Only (black and white)." Print copies of the playlist on colored paper using an inkjet printer.

4. Measure and cut a copy of the playlist to approximately 3¾ x 4 inches. Cut out only the playlist title from one of the copies to use on the front of the insert.

5. Cut a piece of decorative paper to 4¾ x 9½ inches; fold it in half to create a jewel-case insert.

6. Attach the playlist to the back of the insert with photo corners.

7. For the "I Wish You Love" insert, paste strips of decorative paper and trim on the front of the insert. Using an X-acto knife, cut slits on the left and right side of owl's beak; paste the owl to the paper. Using a glue stick, affix the playlist title to the scrap of sheet music, place in the owl's beak, and glue to the paper.

8. For the "Sea Songs" insert, print or photocopy a large letter "S" (approximately 3 inches tall) in black and white. Cut out the letter with an X-acto knife and use the cut-out as a template to trace the "S" onto a piece of sheet music. Cut out the sheet music letter.

9. Layer the sheet music letter on the front of the decorative paper jewel-case insert with other pieces of decorative paper, the playlist title, and a strip of ribbon. Using a glue stick, affix all the pieces of the collage to the insert when they are composed to your liking.

10. Slide the finished jewel case insert into the CD jewel case with the playlist on the inside.

VINTAGE FLASH CARD &  SHEET MUSIC NOTE CARD

Send a happy message by pasting a piece of a vintage flash card, a line of musical lyrics, and lace onto a handmade paper note card.

MATERIALS

Handmade flat card and envelope (Cartiera F. Amatruda Amalfi from Cavallini & Co.), flash card, sheet music, antique bird calling card, lace, Yes! paste, stencil brush, X-acto knife, metal ruler, cutting mat

PROCESS

1. Cut the flash card to fit the flat card.

2. Paste the flash card and a piece of sheet music to the card.

3. Spread paste lightly under the lace and affix to the card.

4. Paste on the bird calling card.

MUSIC-TO-REMEMBER MINI JOURNAL

Choose charming lyrics from a sheet of music to decorate a little journal. Wallpaper trims the edge, and a silk ribbon fastens to a beautiful wooden songbird button to close the booklet. *(See instructions for making mini-journals on page 57.)*

TRACING OUR ROOTS COLLAGE

An evocative family-tree collage combines handmade paper, old journal pages, wallpaper, sheet music, and photographs. Fabric and fiber were used to make the tree; seeds, a map, and words clipped from a garden catalog complete the theme.

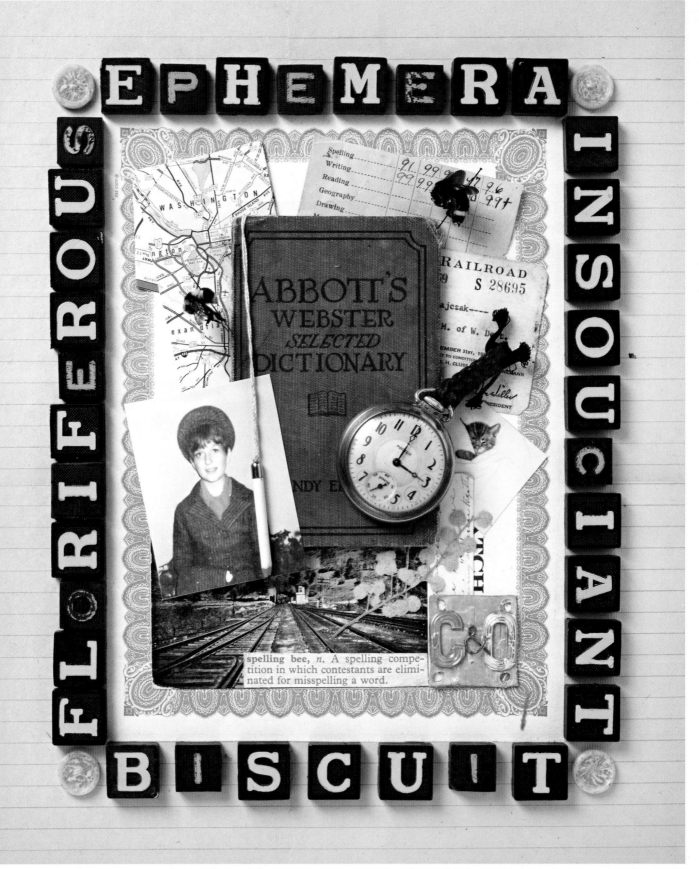

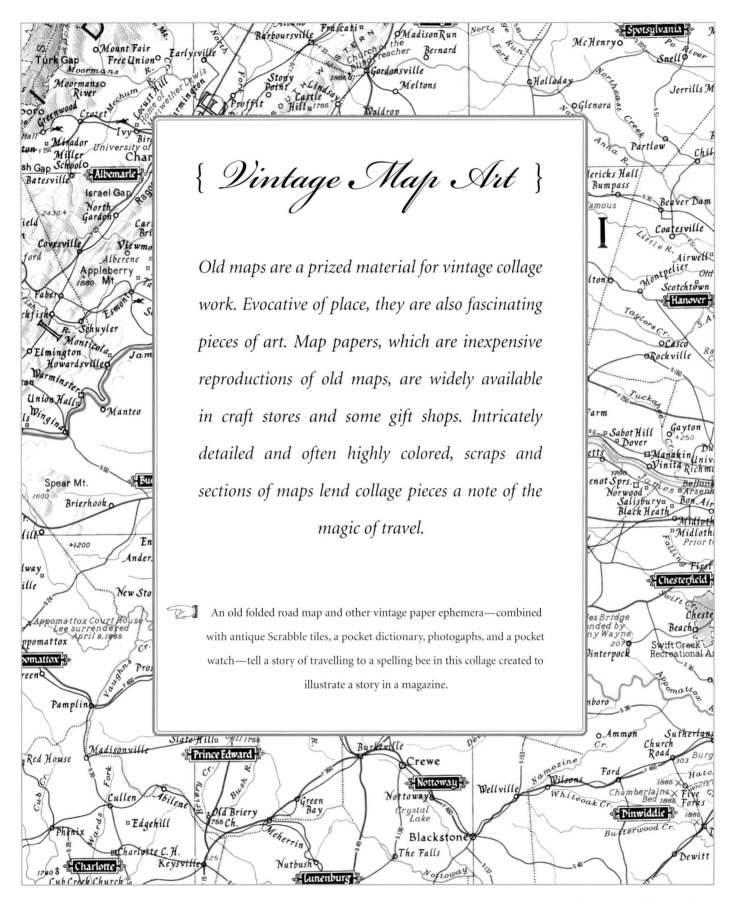

{ *Vintage Map Art* }

Old maps are a prized material for vintage collage work. Evocative of place, they are also fascinating pieces of art. Map papers, which are inexpensive reproductions of old maps, are widely available in craft stores and some gift shops. Intricately detailed and often highly colored, scraps and sections of maps lend collage pieces a note of the magic of travel.

☞ An old folded road map and other vintage paper ephemera—combined with antique Scrabble tiles, a pocket dictionary, photogaphs, and a pocket watch—tell a story of travelling to a spelling bee in this collage created to illustrate a story in a magazine.

 FOLDED MAP NOTE CARD

An antique French envelope, scumbled with watercolor, is mounted onto a note card; the beak of one of the two scrap art birds holds a folded piece of an antique map.

 ITALIAN TRAVEL JOURNAL

A collage that resonates with images and memories of Italy builds on travel journal pages, layering an old photo, a torn map of Italy, scrap art, and decorative trim. An Italian postage stamp, cancellation stamps, and the word *Italy* add to the romantic aura, and scumbled paint unifies the piece as a whole.

MAP-COVERED MEMENTO BOX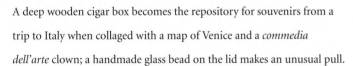

A deep wooden cigar box becomes the repository for souvenirs from a trip to Italy when collaged with a map of Venice and a *commedia dell'arte* clown; a handmade glass bead on the lid makes an unusual pull.

MATERIALS

Deep wooden cigar box, Venician map paper (from Cavallini & Co.), *commedia dell'arte* figure cut from wrapping paper, label, handmade glass bead (from Annabelle Moeller), waxed linen thread, Japanese screw punch, felt, Yes! paste, stencil brush for paste, scissors, X-acto knife, cutting mat, gel medium, old watercolor brush, paper-covered brick

PROCESS

1. Measure and cut the map paper to fit the exterior top and sides of the box. Reserve the borders of the map paper for the edges of the box.

2. Apply paste to the box and affix the paper.

3. Measure and trim the borders of the map paper to fit the edges of the box. Paste on the borders. Paste on the label and figure.

4. Punch a hole in the lid. Insert the linen thread through the hole in the bead, then through the hole in lid. Tie a knot on inside of the lid.

5. Measure and cut the felt to fit the bottom of the box. Paste on the felt and weigh down with the brick until dry.

6. Coat the box entirely with gel medium and let dry.

Map Envelope & Note Card

Scrap art roses embellish these map collages. The entire surface of the envelope, including the elaborately framed address space, is colorfully scumbled, while the note card features a scumbled map with a piece of an antique French envelope and is mounted on card stock.

Materials

Envelope template kit (from Paper Source), pencil, X-acto knife, cutting mat, scissors, antique map or map paper, label, antique rose scrap art, card stock (7 x 10 inches, scored in center), small antique rose scrap art, piece of antique French envelope, piece of map with figure, scrap metal paper (self-adhesive, from Mrs. Grossman's), Yes! paste, stencil brush for paste, Permanent White gouache, scumbling or filbert brush, watercolors and watercolor brushes, paper-covered brick

Process for Envelope

1. Using the envelope kit, make an envelope from an antique map. Paste the label to the front of the envelope.
2. Scumble with Permanent White gouache. Brush watercolors over the entire envelope.
3. Using paste, affix the rose scrap art. Weigh down with the brick until dry.

Process for Card

1. Tear the top edge of the scrap metal paper sheet to make a deckled edge.
2. Measure and cut the bottom and sides of the scrap metal paper sheet to fit the card; affix to the card stock.
3. Using paste, affix the pieces of map and antique envelope and the rose scrap art to the scrap metal paper. Weigh down with the brick until dry.

MAP SKIRT GIRL COLLAGE

A regional map makes a fanciful pleated skirt for a scrap art dance-hall girl; mounted on an old book cover, she has a postage stamp for a hat and a ribbon decorating the top of her colorful skirt.

MATERIALS

Book cover remnant, scrap art girl, map, postage stamp, ribbon, Yes! paste, stencil brush for paste, palette knife, X-acto knife, cutting mat, paper-covered brick

PROCESS

1. Using an X-acto knife, cut the girl's hands away from the original skirt.

2. Spread paste on the scrap art girl, leaving the arms and hands unpasted. Affix her to the book cover remnant and weigh down with the brick to dry.

3. Fold the map into a pleated skirt shape.

4. Paste the top of the map skirt to the girl.

5. Pleat and paste the ribbon to the top of the skirt.

6. Paste the girl's hands on top of the map skirt.

7. Paste the stamp on her head.

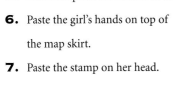

MAP-COVERED MINI JOURNAL

A small notebook becomes a travel journal when collaged with an antique map, an old postage stamp, and a scrap of border from an old stock certificate. Trimmed with gold cord and paper on the spine, it is sealed with a button and waxed linen twine. *(See instructions for making mini-journals on page 57.)*

COLLAGE ON

{ Boxes, Glass, & Metal }

A variety of containers and objects, from old cigar boxes and matchboxes to vintage glass paperweights and metal tins, can be collaged, sealed, and used for utilitarian or decorative purposes. The art of collage can transform the most humble container into a precious work of art. Collaged boxes and glass and metal pieces are especially desirable as gifts; any project in this chapter would be treasured in the home of its lucky recipient.

☞ The lid of a cigar box was used as the base for this beautifully muted collage, which combines an old photograph with a millinery flower, shells, decorative trim, glitter, and a plaster letter. The piece was made to hang on a wall from its antique metallic ribbon.

{ *Cigar Boxes* }

Sturdy yet light, the perfect size to hold letters, jewelry, or mementos, cigar boxes have always been valued for themselves long after their original content has gone up in smoke. They come in a variety of different sizes in both wood and cardboard and are decorated with a stunning array of graphic designs. When using them for collage, cigar boxes can be completely covered with paper to hide their provenance, or you can use the original graphics as part of the collage. The following projects vary— from using the entire box to using just the lid or the bottom—but all of them are exquisitely designed.

FRENCH PAPER–COVERED CIGAR BOX

This deep cigar box is the perfect receptacle for treasures, thanks to its covering of scumbled French map paper and an old French postcard. Trimmed with ribbon and small brass brads, the top is collaged with the image of a woman with a pasted on scalloped label and decorated with a stamped-on Eiffel Tower "hat" lined with glitter.

MATERIALS

Deep cigar box, French map paper (from Cavallini & Co.), Yes! paste, stencil brush for paste, Permanent White gouache, scumbling or filbert brush, other gouache colors, paper photo corners, small brass brads, brown ribbon, pink German glass glitter, glitter adhesive, scalloped card label, ephemera (including card with image of lady with hat and flower), rubber stamp of the Eiffel Tower and ink pad, awl, heavy gel medium, piece of felt for box bottom, scissors, X-acto knife, cutting mat

PROCESS

1. Using a ruler, X-acto knife and cutting mat, measure and cut pieces of the map paper to cover the top and sides of the box. Reserve the border edges of the map paper for the edges of the box.

2. Using paste, affix the map paper to the box top and sides.

3. Scumble on white gouache over the map paper; let dry.

4. Apply thin layers of other gouache colors over white; let dry.

5. Paste border edges of map paper onto box edges.

6. Apply photo corners to the corners of the lid.

7. Using an awl, poke holes in the centers of the photo corners and apply brass brads with paste.

8. Glue on the other ephemera and stamp an Eiffel Tower on the hat.

9. Apply a coat of heavy gel medium over the entire box; let dry.

10. Apply glitter with glitter adhesive to the hat.

11. With scissors, cut felt to the size of the box bottom and apply to the bottom of box with Yes! paste.

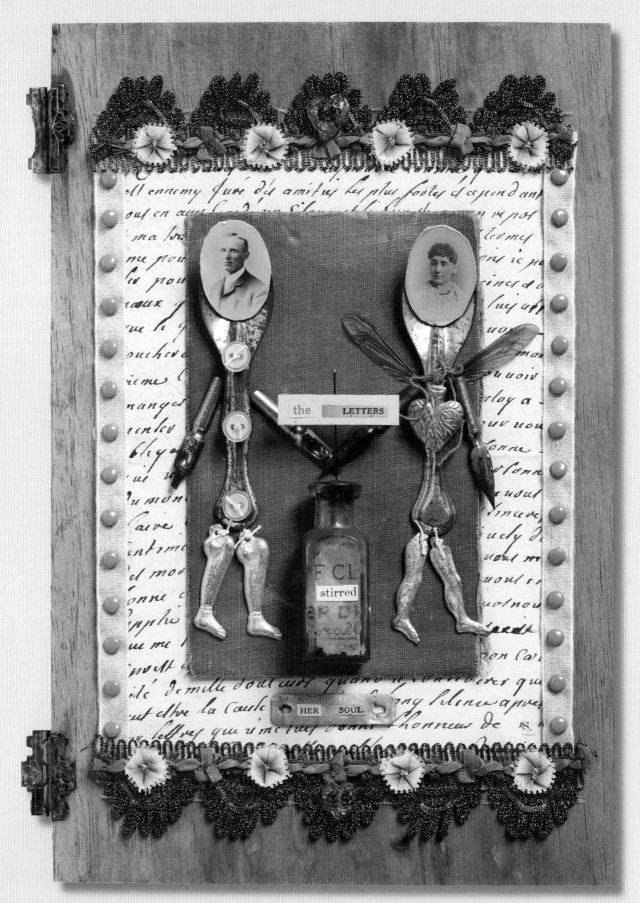

Cigar Box Top Collage

Word clippings send an enigmatic message on this intricately collaged cigar box lid. Decorated with ribbon and brads on the edges, the box also features a heart-shaped button, small spoons, *milagros*, pen nibs, photographs, buttons, insect wings, a pin, a metal label, and even a small bottle.

Materials

Cigar box lid, antique letter, back cover of book, metallic ribbon, flower ribbon, regular ribbon, green brads, green glass heart buttons, child-sized spoons, *milagros* (legs and heart), pen nibs, photographs, buttons, insect wings, bottle, insect pin, construction paper, clippings from booklets, found metal label, thread, Yes! paste, stencil brush for paste, palette knife, floral wire, screwdriver, paper-covered brick, awl, cutting mat

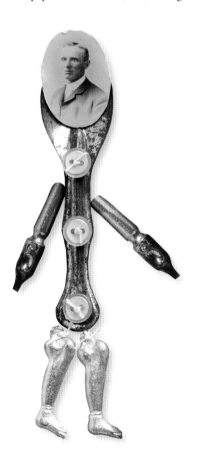

Process

1. Unhinge the cigar box lid with a screwdriver, leaving the hinges on the lid.

2. Mark the placement of the letter on the lid with a pencil; apply paste to the lid and affix the letter.

3. Apply paste to the back of the book cover and affix it to the letter. Weigh down with the brick until dry.

4. Measure the ribbons for the left and right sides. Mark the ribbon with a pencil for the brad placement, insert holes with an awl, and insert the brads in the ribbon holes. Measure the top and bottom ribbons and cut to size.

5. Brush paste on all edges of the letter; affix the ribbons. Affix the heart button to the ribbon at the top with more paste.

6. Knot thread through the holes of the buttons and *milagros* (legs and heart).

7. Using a palette knife, apply paste to the spoons, pen nibs, *milagros* (legs and heart), buttons, and photographs; attach to the collage assembling them into the shapes of a man and woman.

8. Paste the word clippings to the paper label, metal label, and bottle.

9. Pin the paper label to the bottle cork. Using a palette knife, apply paste to the bottle and metal label and affix to the collage.

10. Brush paste lightly on either side of the neck of the spoon woman; then attach the insect wings.

School Days Memento Box

A cigar box is the frame for a school-days collage that groups wooden rulers, a ceramic apple, a report card, rewards of merit, and other scholarly mementos. Scissors, a bottle of gold metal stars, and a pencil complete the motif.

Materials

Cigar box, four wood rulers, velvet ribbon, buttons, ceramic apple, old lined paper, postcard, report card, dictionary page, rewards of merit, booklet, plaster letter A, scissors, glass bottle with cork, gold metal stars, ribbon, tag, pencil, Yes! paste, stencil brush for paste, palette knife, small hand saw, black Micron pen (.005), screwdriver, black tea, mug

Process

1. Unhinge the cigar box lid with a screwdriver; remove the hinges and use bottom of the box.

2. Measure and cut the lined paper to fit the interior bottom of the box. Using a stencil brush, coat the interior bottom of the box with paste and affix the lined paper.

3. Using a pencil, mark the placement of the dictionary page, report card, postcard, and booklet; brush paste within the pencil marks and affix the papers one at a time.

4. Brush paste on the rewards of merit and affix. Using a palette knife, apply paste to the scissors and letter A and affix.

5. Measure and, using a hand saw, cut the rulers to fit the sides of the box.

6. Using a palette knife, apply paste to the outside edge of the cigar box and attach the rulers one by one, propping them up with something until they dry.

7. Measure and cut the velvet ribbon to fit the outside edge of the box next to the rulers; using a palette knife, apply paste to the inside edge of the rulers and attach the ribbon. Apply paste to the buttons and affix to the ribbons.

8. Make a cup of black tea and soak the white tag to the desired color; dry on paper. Using a pen, write "Gold Stars" on the tag.

9. Fill the bottle with stars. Tie the tag around the bottle neck with thin ribbon, apply paste to the bottom of the bottle with a palette knife, and affix the bottle to the box.

10. Using a palette knife, apply paste to the apple and pencil; affix to the box.

{ *Small Boxes* }

*M*atchboxes and other small, sturdy paper boxes can be put to attractive use through collage. Boxes are available in gift and craft stores, but you can also use empty note card, stationery, and gift boxes that you've saved. Cutting a window in the lid of a small paper box and collaging the exterior and interior creates a charming dioramic container to hold mementos of a trip or a special place. And collaging matchboxes and filling each one with a tiny gift or personalized message makes inventive and memorable place cards.

DIORAMA BOXES

Two boxes with a nautical theme show off a collection of sea treasures: The hinged lid of the box on the left is trimmed with marbled paper and decorative gold edging, while the interior holds paper ephemera, a map, and found objects from nature such as stones, beach glass, and seaweed. The lid is tied shut with a gold-painted seashell. The large matchbox on the right is covered with marbled paper and reveals a collection of shells on a scrap art background inside.

MATCHBOX PLACE CARDS

Your guests will be charmed by these keepsake place cards with messages written in walnut stain ink and collaged with stamps and scrap art. Each opens to disclose a line of poetry and a tiny gift of a flower, feather, stone, or other natural object.

MATERIALS

Small matchboxes, Yes! paste, stencil brush for paste, marbled paper, Permanent White gouache, scumbling or filbert brush, watercolors and watercolor brushes, ephemera (including scrap art and stamps), small scalloped-edged cards, calligraphy pen, Sennelier walnut stain ink, natural objects for matchboxes to match quotes (flowers, feathers, small stones, etc.), X-acto knife, cutting mat, bar of soap

PROCESS

1. Measure and cut a piece of marbled paper to cover the tops and sides of the box tops.

2. Using paste, affix the paper to the box tops. Paste on stamps and scrap art.

3. Paint the inside of the box tops with white gouache; let dry.

4. Paint the inside of the box bottoms with white gouache; let dry. Paint washes of watercolors over the gouache; let dry.

5. Rub the edges of the box bottoms with a bar of soap so they will slide in and out of the tops easily.

6. Write a quote or poem on each scalloped card with the pen and ink; place a card inside each box along with a natural object related to the message; slide the box bottoms into the tops and place a box at each place setting.

"New hope may bloom, and days may come,

{ *Glass & Terra-Cotta* }

*O*ld glass has a particular romance: antique molded bottles of cloudy glass, hand-blown glass with imperfections and bubbles. Minimally collaged to let the pleasing shape and translucency of the glass show through, the following projects turn old glass into ornamented containers or objets d'art. Terra-cotta pots, with their classic shape and earthy color, also become decorative containers through the art of collage.

GLITTER SHAKERS

Old glass salt and pepper shakers with patinated tops become shakers for German glass glitter when decorated with ribbons, glittery labels made from French flash cards, and old rhinestone buttons.

MATERIALS

Glass or crystal salt and pepper shakers, old rhinestone buttons, ribbons, vintage bullion angel hair, French flash cards, German glass glitter, glitter adhesive and thin metal aplicator tip, X-acto knife, metal ruler, cutting mat, Japanese screw punch

PROCESS

1. Fill the salt and pepper shakers with glitter.

2. Measure and cut the flash cards into tags.

3. Punch a hole at the left edge of each tag.

4. Using the glitter adhesive and the metal tip, apply a thin edge of adhesive to the sides of a tag. Sprinkle with glitter and let dry. Repeat for each tag.

5. Wrap angel hair around the top of one or more of the bottles, if desired. Thread ribbons through the buttons and tags; tie one of each to each bottle.

BLUE BOTTLE COLLAGE

Collage an old blue-glass bottle to serve as a paperweight or *objet d'art* by circling it with an elaborate antique belt buckle and ribbon; top the buckle with an image cut from a photograph, a millinery flower, and a song lyric clipping.

SHELL JAR

A filmy glass jar holds a collection of small shells and a piece of mermaid scrap art; the knot of a ribbon tied around the jar is affixed with sealing wax, and the vellum label is pasted over the ends of the ribbon on the side of the jar.

GLASS PAPERWEIGHT COLLAGES

Empty glass paperweights become magical objects when their interiors are filled with collaged ephemera—an old postcard, stamps, scrap art, pieces of old letters, a butterfly—and sealed with backing.

MATERIALS

Empty glass paperweights, ephemera (including old letters, scrap art, stamps, a postcard, and a butterfly), Yes! paste, stencil brush for paste; X-acto knife, cutting mat, thin piece of museum board or piece of heavy (140-lb.) watercolor paper for backing, felt, glitter adhesive, scissors, paper-covered brick

PROCESS

1. Using an X-acto knife, cut a piece of board to fit the paperweight.

2. Paste ephemera in a design on the board.

3. Apply a small amount of paste around the edge of the board and affix it to the paperweight.

4. Using scissors, cut a piece of felt to fit the paperweight and paste it on the bottom. Weigh down with the brick until dry.

COLLAGE ON TERRA-COTTA POTS

The pleasing, sturdy shapes of old terra-cotta pots are transformed into containers for art and craft supplies through the art of collage. The scumbled pot on the left is decorated with scrap art and rubber-stamped with bird images; the pot on the right features a collaged medallion tied onto the pot with ribbon.

MATERIALS

Old terra-cotta pots, Yes! paste, stencil brush for paste; (*for scrap art pot*) gouache paints, scumbling or filbert brush, bird rubber stamp, Versa Magic archival multi-surface chalk "Jumbo Java" brown ink pad, scrap art, ribbon, metallic string; (*for pot with medallion*) metal frame, bird trading card, letter B from sewing pattern tissue, word clipping from music book, wide silk ribbon, thin strong ribbon, glue stick, circle template, scissors

PROCESS FOR SCRAP ART POT

1. Using the brown ink pad, rubber-stamp birds on the pot.

2. Scumble gouache on the pot to give it an antique look.

3. Using Yes! paste, affix the scrap art. Paste ribbon and metallic string around the bottom edge of the pot.

PROCESS FOR MEDALLION POT

1. Tie a length of wide ribbon around the pot and knot it in the front.

2. Using a circle template, cut out a bird image slightly larger than the diameter of the metal frame opening.

3. Apply glue stick to the letter B and word clipping, and affix both to the bird image.

4. Using paste, affix the collage to the back of the frame.

5. Tie thin ribbons to both sides of the frame, wrap it around the pot, and tie it in the back.

{ *Metal* }

The smooth surface of metal takes easily to collage, opening the door to a new category of objects to be transformed. Metal tins are the most obvious, from antique tea tins and used cookie tins to new tins purchased from gifts and craft stores. Look for metal embroidery and paint stencil letters and old tintypes at antique stores and flea markets as another way to personalize a collage using metal ephemera.

METAL STENCIL MINI-JOURNAL

Collage a booklet with decorative papers and wide ribbon; then personalize it with a metal stencil letter sewn to its cover. Use an awl to make holes in the stencil and journal cover for the needle and thread. (*See instructions for making mini-journals on page 57.*)

COLLAGED TEA TINS

Recycled tea tins, collaged and filled with loose or bagged tea, are perfect gifts for your tea-loving friends. The tin on the left is decorated with paper lace and a leaf ribbon holding a tag; the top is ornamented with a photograph and a glitter-edged leaf. The tin on the right is collaged with ephemera, including a Dresden elephant, postage stamp, and a tag; the top is decorated with fragrant cloves and spicy peppercorns.

MATERIALS

Recycled matcha tea tins, circle template, Yes! paste, stencil brush for paste, scissors, leaf ribbon, small paper tags, black Micron pen (.005); (*for chai tea tin*) ephemera (including scrap of letter, stamp from India, and Dresden elephant), metallic string, scrap metal design lines (self-adhesive, from Mrs. Grossman's), whole cloves, and peppercorns; (*for green tea tin*) scrap of letter, photograph, dried leaf, paper lace, German glass glitter, palette knife, acrylic matte varnish, old small watercolor brush for varnish, glitter adhesive with thin metal applicator tip, black tea, tea mug

PROCESS FOR CHAI TEA TIN

1. Using a circle template, cut out the scrap of letter to fit the lid of the tin; cut out another piece of letter to wrap around the bottom sides of tin. Using paste, affix all the pieces to tin.

2. Paste the stamp on top of the letter on the lid.

3. Paste metallic string around the edge of the lid; paste the cloves and peppercorns in a circle next to the string.

4. Apply the scrap metal lines to the top and bottom of the letter around the side of tin.

5. Tie the leaf ribbon around the tin; paste the elephant over the ribbon.

6. Inscribe the tag with the name of the tea using a black pen, and tie the tag to the ribbon with metallic string.

PROCESS FOR GREEN TEA TIN

1. Coat the dried leaf with matte acrylic varnish and let dry.

2. Using a circle template, cut out the letter and photograph.

3. Using a stencil brush, apply paste to the tin and affix the letter; repeat to affix the photograph to the letter.

4. Using glitter adhesive and the metal tip, apply a thin edge of adhesive to the leaf; sprinkle with glitter and let dry.

5. Measure the paper lace to fit around the tin. Brush paste around the bottom of the tin and affix the lace; paste the seam closed.

6. Make a cup of black tea, soak the white tag to the desired color, and let it dry on paper. Cut the tag into a leaf shape and inscribe it with the name of the tea, using a black pen.

7. Tie the leaf ribbon with the tag around the tin.

8. Using a palette knife, apply paste to the dried leaf and affix it to the photograph to look like a woman's hat.

METAL KEEPSAKE TIN WITH SCRAP ART COLLAGE

Collaged with scrap art, small metal tins—perfect for holding buttons, pins, and other tiny objects—are fascinating objects in their own right.

COLLAGE ON ANTIQUE TINS

Old metal tins, distressed by time and use, have a nostalgic appeal that is enhanced by collage. The tin at left on the facing page has a scrap art owl pasted under a metal stencil letter O; the tin at top, perfect for holding art pens and writing utensils, is decorated with a tintype photograph, the heads of furniture nails, and ribbon edging; a beribboned pen nib is glued to the lid. The tin at right combines decorative paper, ribbon, cord, an antique rabbit card, and glitter to make a container for Easter treats.

MATERIALS FOR OWL TIN

Rusted tin, metal stencil letter O, scrap art owl, scissors, silk ribbon, Yes! paste, stencil brush for paste

PROCESS

1. Measure and cut the owl scrap to fit behind the stencil.
2. Using Yes! paste, coat the back of the stencil and affix it to the owl. Coat the back of the owl and the stencil and affix them to the top of the tin.
3. Measure and cut a piece of ribbon to tie in a bow around the tin.

MATERIALS FOR PEN NIB TIN

Rusted tin, tintype photograph, scrap of letter, ribbon edging, thin ribbon, scissors, antique brass furniture nails, pen nib, Yes! paste, stencil brush for paste, palette knife, wire cutter, paper-covered brick

PROCESS

1. Measure the scrap of letter to fit the lid of the tin and mark the placement on the lid with a pencil.
2. Brush paste on the lid inside the placement marks and affix the letter.

3. Coat the back of the photograph with paste, affix it to the letter, and weigh it down with the brick until dry.
4. Measure and cut the ribbon trim; place the trim on the edge of the letter. Using a wire cutter, cut off the tops of the nails. Using a palette knife, fill the undersides of the nail tops with paste and affix them to the trim and letter.
5. Measure, cut, and tie a ribbon around the pen nib. Using a palette knife, apply paste to the underside of the nib, and press it on the photograph (to resemble a woman's hat).

MATERIALS FOR RABBIT TIN

Round blank tin, decorative paper, scrap metal design lines (self-adhesive, from Mrs. Grossman's), velvet ribbon, gold cord, artificial flower stamens, glitter, ribbon flower bow, antique rabbit card, felt, Yes! paste, stencil brush for paste, glitter adhesive, scissors

PROCESS

1. Cut a round of decorative paper to fit the lid of the tin; paste it to the lid.
2. Apply the scrap metal lines to the sides of the lid and bottom of the tin.
3. Cut a circle (smaller in diameter than the lid and decorative paper) from the rabbit card and paste it in the center of the lid.
4. Paste velvet ribbon around the edges of the tin lid and bottom.
5. Paste the gold cord next to the velvet ribbon on the lid and bottom of the tin; paste the flower stamens to the gold cord only around the lid of the tin.
6. Apply glitter around the edge of the rabbit card with glitter adhesive.
7. Paste the ribbon flower bow to the rabbit.
8. Measure and cut the felt to fit the tin bottom; paste felt to the bottom.

Rose petal tea

TEA

S.

COLLAGE WITH

{*Nature*}

The natural world is rich with materials for collage: Flowers, leaves, feathers, bark, seeds, seashells, and rocks may all be used alone or in combination with other materials to create magical works. Most of these objects are found in nature, though feathers, rocks, eggs, and shells may also be purchased in craft stores. Collage with natural ephemera lends itself to creating particularly beautiful and sometimes whimsical works.

Shown are some of the many ways to use natural materials in collage: a bookmark made from a flash card, part of a letter, a photograph, and pressed rose petals; a stone paperweight with an overall collage of letter scraps, postage stamps, and cancellation marks, and another with a strip of lace and a postage stamp; and a journal collaged with lace, part of a letter, and a preserved green leaf.

{ *Pressed Botanicals* }

*P*reserved leaves, flowers, and even seaweed are perfect for collage work suitable for framing or freestanding sculptural pieces, but they also add beauty and depth to objects meant for daily use. When dried correctly, they retain their shape and much of their color, and when preserved with a coating of varnish, they will last indefinitely if not exposed to strong light.

PRESSED-FLOWER BOOKMARK
MATERIALS

Flash card, photograph, scrap of letter, scrap of wallpaper, pressed rose petals, metallic trim, Yes! paste, stencil brush for paste, PVA adhesive, acrylic matte varnish, old watercolor brush for PVA and varnish, X-acto knife, cutting mat, metal ruler, paper-covered brick, toothpick

PROCESS

1. Measure and cut the photograph to fit the flash card.

2. Make light pencil marks for the placement of the photograph on the flash card, brush the flash card with paste, and attach the photograph. Repeat Steps 1 and 2 for the scraps of letter and wallpaper; weigh down with the brick until dry.

4. One at a time, carefully brush PVA adhesive onto the back of the rose petals and affix them to the photograph; using an old brush, coat the petals with varnish.

5. Measure and draw a pencil line on the flash card for the trim, apply a thin line of paste with a toothpick, and press the trim to the card.

PRESSED FLOWER COLLAGE

A rose-themed collage is made of old lined paper, a letter, and clippings from an old garden catalog and fashion magazine; wooden garden stakes become the frame, and a metal rose tag and rose ephemera—the pressed flower and leaves, seeds, and thorns—play out the theme.

Seaweed comes in a wide variety of forms and makes a delicate and unusual addition to any collage. Shapes range from fans to branching coral to streamers, and colors run the gamut from pale greens and yellows to warm rusts, reds, and pinks. Use seaweed along with shells and beach scenes for ocean-themed collages, or paste it onto to old papers and other vintage materials to add color and texture. Take care when pressing and preserving seaweed, as it is quite fragile.

PRESSED SEAWEED & DOCUMENT COLLAGE

Lacy pressed seaweed collaged over a painted fan-shaped seaweed add visual interest and texture to a scumbled old document edged with Italian marbled paper.

LEAVES, BARK, & SEEDS COLLAGE

An elaborate collage combines family-tree imagery with the boot of Italy made from bark. Seeds, lichen, dried leaves, and clippings from a gardening booklet and a seed packet emphasize the botanical and Italian roots of this artwork.

MATERIALS

Handmade paper, antique journal pages, Italian postcard, clipping from gardening booklet, clipping from map, glassine envelope, dirt, clipping from seed packet, seeds, tree bark, lichen, scrap art tree, dried leaves, photographs, alphabet pasta, low-tack tape, Yes! paste, stencil brush for paste, acrylic matte varnish, old watercolor brush for varnish, palette knife, toothpick, heavy book

PROCESS

1. Using a pencil, mark the placement of the journal pages on the handmade paper; brush paste on the handmade paper and affix the pages to the paper.

2. Brush paste on the postcard, "root" paper clipping, and map. Affix and weigh down with a book until dry.

3. Rub the glassine envelope in dirt to roughen and age the surface. Paste the "seeds" clipping on the envelope, fill with seeds, tape closed, and paste onto the postcard.

4. Using an old brush, coat the leaves, lichen, bark, and pasta letters with varnish and let dry.

5. Using a stencil brush and paste, affix the tree-top scrap art. Using a palette knife and paste, affix the leaves, lichen, bark, and photographs, placing the pieces of bark and lichen into the shape of the boot of Italy.

6. Using a toothpick and paste, affix the pasta letters to spell "ITALY."

NATURE PORTRAIT COLLAGE

An altered photograph of Frida Kahlo becomes a portrait of the artist as a nature goddess interpreted in botanicals—with an aura of seedpods, a dried flower head for hair, a butterfly on her shoulder, an antique paintbrush, and other botanicals including flowers petals and dried rose thorns.

SEEDS

Cartolina

ITALY

Sicily is beautiful. It is Spring here and the whole place is carpeted with wild flowers. Great huge purple flowers they call anemones. The almond trees are all in bloom and things

tannery it removed from the tan. Few weeds came up through this heavy mulch, but the grapes push up readily. Many varieties grow well by this method, while others are scattering, only here and there a plant, but with new varieties there is a great gain in getting double the number of cuttings. Under glass nurserymen propagate from single eyes cut from two to three inches long, started in shallow boxes of sand, and afterwards potted or transplanted in beds. A good way to increase a valuable variety is to graft single eye cuttings on grape roots and plant in the usual way. Grafting is now practiced more largely than ever

NATURE DIORAMA COLLAGE

This dramatic collage offers a glimpse into the past as envisioned in a cigar-box diorama crowned by millinery leaves: Tree bark, lichen, a June beetle, field grass, and jasmine tea pearls frame old family photographs set in nature.

MATERIALS

Cigar box (bottom), decorative paper, thin ribbon, beetle buttons, tree bark, millinery leaves, lichen, field grass (for models/hobbies), jasmine pearl green tea, hemp twine, scroll pin, photographs, paper word clippings, preserved June beetle, Yes! paste, stencil brush for paste, PVA adhesive, acrylic matte varnish, old watercolor brush for varnish, palette knife, cardboard, dark brown acrylic paint, acrylic brush, X-acto knife, metal ruler, cutting mat

PROCESS

1. Paint the interior walls and facing edges of the cigar box bottom with brown acrylic paint; let dry.

3. Coat the tree bark, lichen, June beetle, and jasmine pearls with acrylic matte varnish; let dry.

4. Measure and cut the decorative paper to fit the background of the box. Brush paste on the box and affix the paper. Paste thin ribbon around the edges of the box.

5. Cut small square cardboard props for support of the tree trunks. Paste to the box, one at a time, until the trunks are supported; then paste and attach the trunks to the supports.

6. Cut a blunt edge on the hobby grass. Put adhesive on the box next to the base of the tree trunks and affix the grass in clumps on the cut side.

7. Using a palette knife and paste, affix the leaves, lichen, buttons, beetle, jasmine pearls, and photographs.

8. Paste the word clippings "tree" and "love" to the scroll, then tie the scroll to the tree trunk with hemp twine.

PRESSED-LEAF GARDEN JOURNAL

Choose a green cloth-bound booklet to collage into a garden journal by layering it with a name card, lace, postage stamps, a hand *milagro*, and an elegantly shaped pressed leaf.

{ *Rocks & Shells* }

Rocks and shells are nature's own sculptures, needing little embellishment to enhance their beauty. Small shells and stones can be incorporated into collages and sealed with acrylic varnish. The elegant shapes and varied textures of these natural sculptures make them perfect for use as paperweights and containers to be filled with carefully chosen treasures.

ROCK COLLAGE PAPERWEIGHT

A large, oval river rock is just right for weighing down a stack of papers. The colorful all-over collage is made up of ephemera, including stamps, pieces of letters and maps. The smaller paperweight lets the outside of the rock show through and is festooned with a scrap of lace and wallpaper, and topped with beautiful bird postage stamp.

MATERIALS

River rocks, Yes! paste, stencil brush for paste, heavy gel medium, Brilliant Gold gouache, watercolor brush, rubber cancellation stamps and ink pads, old lace, and ephemera (including stamps, pieces of letters, maps, and wallpaper)

PROCESS

1. For the large rock, using paste, affix the ephemera to the rock.

2. Stamp with cancellation marks.

3. Brush on Brilliant Gold gouache.

4. Brush the entire rock with heavy gel medium to seal.

5. For the small rock, wrap lace around the rock, with the seam on top.

6. Using paste, affix the wallpaper and stamp on top of the seam.

COLLAGE IN SHELL

The mother-of-pearl interior of an abalone shell provides the perfect container for a collage with a photograph and a postage stamp; a beach-themed line of type and a crab pincer emphasize the ocean motif.

STARFISH PAPERWEIGHT

An elegantly restrained paperweight lets the natural beauty of the starfish shine, ornamented only with a small photograph, a ribbon, and a dragonfly fishing lure.

MATERIALS

Starfish, wide silk ribbon, thin ribbon, photograph, dragonfly fishing lure, Yes! paste, stencil brush, pinking shears

PROCESS

1. Measure a piece of wide ribbon to fit over the body of the starfish; cut the ends with pinking shears.

2. Using a stencil brush and paste, affix the ribbon to the starfish.

3. Using a stencil brush and paste, affix the photograph to the ribbon.

4. Measure and cut a piece of thin ribbon to wrap and tie around the starfish. Hook the fishing lure on the thin ribbon at the bow.

Note: If you set the collage elements on the starfish without using paste, you can change them as you like.

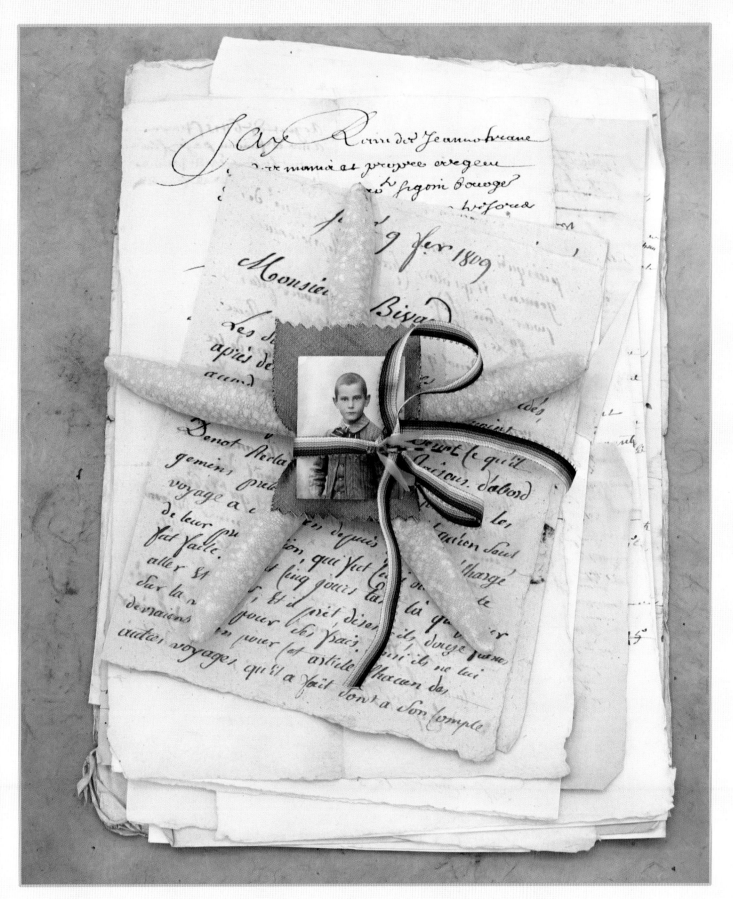

{ *Bird Ephemera* }

Storebought nests, eggshells, and feathers are iconic bird ephemera from nature to build a collage around or to use as the final whimsical touch to a collaged piece. Combine them with other natural objects, or contrast them with manufactured materials like scrap art, photographs, or ribbons. Whether you find them in nature or on the shelves of a nature shop or craft store, these earthly gifts will add a note of nature's artistry to your own creations.

EGG & NEST CIGAR BOX COLLAGE

An antique photograph of a baby, mounted on old and handmade papers, is the family heirloom inside a cigar box with a sliding top; a quail egg, small feathers, and a nest handmade of natural fiber and lichen resonate with the playful words hanging by hooks and eyes from the top of the box.

MATERIALS

Cigar box with sliding lid (bottom), handmade paper, found old paper, wide velvet ribbon, photograph, store bought quail egg, domesticated small feathers, natural fiber, lichen, paper card, hooks and eyes, buttons, needle and thread, found small piece of cardboard, paper word clippings from a cookbook ("A," "good," "egg"), muslin, Yes! paste, stencil brush for paste, acrylic matte varnish, old watercolor brush for varnish, palette knife, needle, X-acto knife, metal ruler, cutting mat, paper-covered brick, small book to fit inside box

PROCESS

1. Measure and cut the handmade paper to fit the inside bottom of the box. Brush paste in the box and affix the paper.

2. Using paste, affix the piece of old paper, velvet ribbon, and photograph to the handmade paper; then weigh down with a book and the brick until dry.

3. Using an X-acto knife, carefully cut the egg in half crosswise.

4. Using an old brush, coat the outside of the egg with varnish.

5. Apply paste to the muslin and stuff it into the egg to affix. Using a palette knife and paste, affix the egg to the photograph.

6. Arrange the fibers and lichen into a nest. Using a palette knife and paste, affix the nest to the box.

7. Brush paste on the paper in the box and affix the feathers.

8. Using a needle and thread, sew buttons and hooks to the cardboard; using a palette knife and paste, affix the cardboard to the box.

9. Sew eyes to the small piece of cardboard; brush paste on the word clippings and affix to the cardboard; hook the cardboard to the box.

TOOTH FAIRY COLLAGE

Create a fantastical tooth fairy using an old photograph, handmade paper, fabric swatches, star buttons, a model tooth, and pearl beads. A magazine clipping forms the arms and legs, while white feathers become the fairy's sleeves and skirt and adorn her hat and shoes.

FEATHERED SONGBIRD CLIPS

Bird shapes cut from sheet music backed with decorative paper are trimmed with fancy feathers and buttons. Glued onto the tops of wooden clothespins, the birds become clips to hold photographs onto an artistic clothesline.

MATERIALS

Sheet music, decorative paper, lightweight buttons, embroidery or metallic thread (or thin ribbon), domesticated bird feathers, wooden clothespins, Yes! paste, stencil brush for paste, awl, X-acto knife, cutting mat, needle, small piece of thin cardboard, pencil

PROCESS

1. Make a bird stencil: On thin cardboard, draw a bird shape and cut it out with an X-acto knife (you will use cardboard with empty bird shape as a stencil).

2. Place the bird stencil over the music sheet and trace with a pencil.

3. Cut out the music bird and brush paste on the back; affix the bird to a small piece of decorative paper.

4. Cut the bird out with a border of decorative paper surrounding it.

5. Place a button on the tail; using a pencil, mark the placement of the buttonholes on the paper.

6. Using an awl, make holes in the paper. Using paste and a brush, affix the feathers between holes. Using a needle and thread, sew the button on the tail and tie the thread in a bow.

7. Brush paste on top of the clothespin and affix it to the bird.

 ## FEATHER IN AN ALTERED BOOK

An old Italian book is altered into book art with the addition of a flamboyant feather, an antique journal clipping, and a transfer on an Italian book page.

FEATHERED NOTE CARDS

Antique cards and French letters were scumbled with paint and jaunty bird feathers were added to the hats for these note cards. *(See pages 38–39 for creating scumbled antique postcards.)*

Raport fait
les travaux
de reboisement
fait, dans le
canton de
Cunlhat

Commissaires
m.m. Mory
et Bastier
Deroure, rapporteur

À Monsieur le président
De la Société D'agriculture
Du puy-de-Dôme

Par Votre lettre en date du 4 juillet dernier Vous
avez nommé Commissaires m.m. Mory de Cunlhat,
Et Bastier Deroure habitant à Chalandrat même
Commune, pour présenter un Raport à la Société,
Sur La Situation des travaux de reboisement
Effectués par elle, conjointement avec l'administration
forestière de ce département.

Votre Commission réduite à un Seul membre, pour
une absence obligée, de mr Mory, S'est transportée
Successivement Sur les parties de Communaux
Soumises au régime forestier, Situés dans les
Communes de Cunlhat Et d'auzelle, En S. faisant
accompagner par le Sr Bodow gard. forestier.
L'inspection a été commencée Sur le communal
Dit de jeannot, dont la contenance Seulement de
Cinq hectares Soumise, il en a qu'un hectare trois ares
Ensemencé En pins Silvestre et épicéa, Ces
Derniers n'ont pas réussi.
Les Semis de 1846 avaient laissé des Vacants
que ceux des années Suivantes ont très bien
Réparés, les plants Sont En général beaux, Vigoureux
Et même trop rapprochés les uns des autres, excepté
Sur une très petite Surface de la partie orientale où

GEN. DE CAEN
VINGTS

L'an mil Sept cents Soixante
Cinq Le Douzieme jour D'avril à Sahanville
Devant Nous Guillaume Charles Morlet
Notaire Royal de Sanssuo & Dependance
Soussigné M---

Fut present Enpersonne Le Sieur
françois Charles Davy Ecuyer delaparoisse
De Gatteville y demeurant, ayant Epouzé
Demoiselle ô Dame Madeleine de Xeuve
fille & heritiere defeu Sieur Jacques de
Xeuve Ecuyer delaparoisse de Sainte
Geneviève, Lequel en Cette qualité a Baillé
quitté, Cedé et delaissé à titre de fieffe pure
Simple, perpetuelle & irevocable fait sur
& Les Biens ou ayants Cause, Bienspromesse
Des parcutien fournir & faire Vallode detous
troubles & Empeichements Generallement
quelconque, au profit & De ce fait du Sieur
Davy authorise de Erman Ecuyer Sieur
De Louville dela paroisse de Digosville
un B

{ Clip Art }

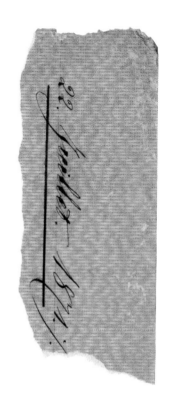

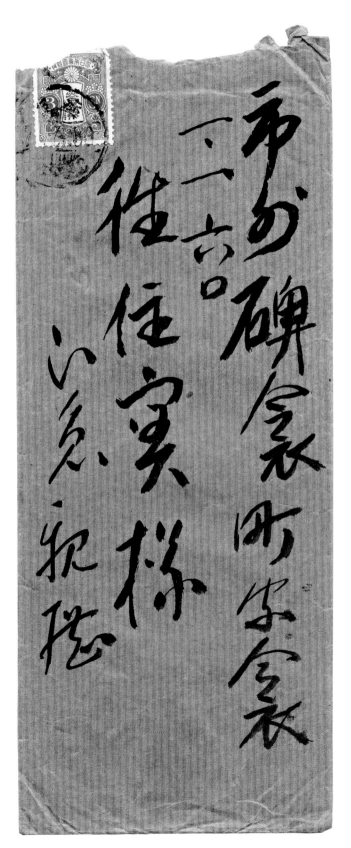

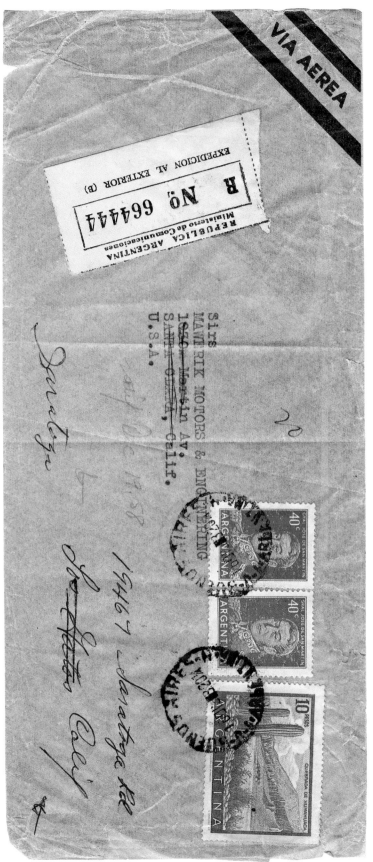

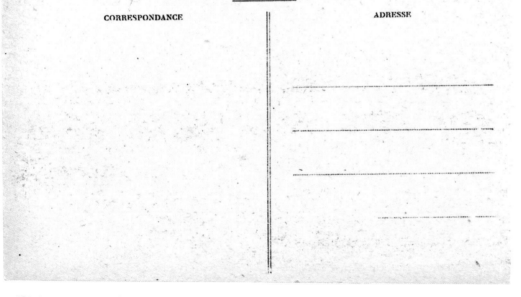

FIRENZE - *Ponte Vecchio e altri ponti.*

Vue générale de l'Ancienne Abbaye d'HAUTVILLERS
Propriété de la Maison Moët et Chandon

{ Clip Art }

Prothonotary Warbler

Dickcissel

Painted Bunting

Varied Bunting

126'
looked

J. W. STORM,
DENTIST,
Uses Vitalized Air for Painless Extraction of Teeth. All work warranted first class in every respect. Office over Button & Munsell's.

PRICE & KNICKERBOCKER,
Seedsmen,
ALBANY, - - - - N. Y.
ILLUSTRATED CATALOGUE ISSUED FEB. 1st.

Eggs of Bullfinch.

AU BON DIABLE
39, rue de Rivoli

RESPECTEZ VOS SUPÉRIEURS

Eggs of Redstart

{ *Resources* }

Most of the materials and tools listed below are available in art and craft stores, but they can often also be ordered directly from the manufacturer. Look for vintage materials such as stamps, postcards, letters, and wallpaper trim at flea markets, antiques stores, paper fairs, and second-hand shops and on the Internet; new and reproduced materials are available in craft stores and on the Internet.

Art Institute Glitter, Inc.
712 North Balboa Street
Cottonwood, AZ 86326
877-909-0805
www.artglitter.com
Art Glitter Designer Dries Clear adhesive, ultrafine metal tips, vintage glass glitter (fine and shards).

Avery Dennison
50 Pointe Drive
Brea, CA 92821
800-462-8379
www.avery.com
Matte White CD/DVD Labeling System (Ink Jet 8965: disc labels, jewel-case inserts, applicator, software), white marking tags, jewelry tags.

Bell'occhio
8 Brady Street
San Francisco, CA 94103
415-864-4048
www.bellocchio.com
Teenie Scallopini small scallop-edged cards, ribbon, millinery trim.

Bonny Doon Mercantile
www.bdmercantile.com
Handmade glass beads.

Cavallini & Co.
401 Forbes Boulevard
South San Francisco, CA 94080
800-226-5287
www.cavallini.com
Cartiera F. Amatruda Amalfi handmade flat cards and envelopes, decorative wrap, map papers.

Daniel Smith
4150 First Avenue South
Seattle, WA 98124
800-426-6740
www.danielsmith.com
Watercolors (Sennelier), gouache paints (Winsor & Newton, Daler-Rowney), oxgall (Daniel Smith), matte medium (Golden), walnut stain ink (Sennelier shellac-based ink), Pigma Micron ink pens (.005), Indian Village 100% cotton rag handmade watercolor paper, special papers, awls, Japanese screw punches, bone folders, Yes! paste, Lineco Neutral pH Adhesive (PVA adhesive in bottles), Simply Simmons scumbling brushes, palette knives.

Dover Publications
www.doverpublications.com
Clip art in books (Pictorial Archive).

EK Success
www.eksuccess.com
Jolee's Boutique Corner Embellishments Gold Accents (SPJD001).

Koch Studios: Maryjo & Sunny Koch
maryjo@kochstudios.com
sunny@kochstudios.com
www.kochstudios.com
Portfolios, prints, cards, classes.

Liquitex
www.liquitex.com
Acrylic matte varnish.

Mrs. Grossman's
P.O. Box 4467
Petaluma, CA 94955
800-429-4549
www.mrsgrossmans.com
Scrap metal paper in three sizes: design line, full sheet, and giant.

Paper Source
Stores nationwide
888-PAPER-11
www.paper-source.com
Yes! paste, PVA adhesive (in jars), glue sticks, awls, bone folders, Soft Grip razor knives, paste brushes, rubber stamps, Versa Magic Chalk inkpads, envelope template kits, papers (such as small green batik dots, cream and green Italian leaf prints).

Scrapbook Adhesives by 3L
www.scrapbook-adhesives.com
Self-adhesive photo corners (classic style).

Victorian Scrap Works
777-314-2250
www.victorianscrapworks.com
Dresden trims, scrap art.

Vintage Paper Fair
415-668-1636
www.vintagepaperfair.com
Scrap art, postcards, papers.

{ *Index* }

{ Notes }

{ *Metric Conversions* }

inches to millimeters and centimeters

inches	mm	cm	inches	cm	inches	cm
⅛	3	0.3	9	22.9	30	76.2
¼	6	0.6	10	25.4	31	78.7
½	13	1.3	12	30.5	33	83.8
⅝	16	1.6	13	33.0	34	86.4
¾	19	1.9	14	35.6	35	88.9
⅞	22	2.2	15	38.1	36	91.4
1	25	2.5	16	40.6	37	94.0
1¼	32	3.2	17	43.2	38	96.5
1½	38	3.8	18	45.7	39	99.1
1¾	44	4.4	19	48.3	40	101.6
2	51	5.1	20	50.8	41	104.1
2½	64	6.4	21	53.3	42	106.7
3	76	7.6	22	55.9	43	109.2
3½	89	8.9	23	58.4	44	111.8
4	102	10.2	24	61.0	45	114.3
4½	114	11.4	25	63.5	46	116.8
5	127	12.7	26	66.0	47	119.4
6	152	15.2	27	68.6	48	121.9
7	178	17.8	28	71.1	49	124.5
8	203	20.3	29	73.7	50	127.0

mm - millimeters   cm - centimeters

CREDITS

Collage Projects by Maryjo Koch:
Pages 2, 5, 16–19, 24, 29, 30–31, 35–43, 48–52, 56, 57 (bottom), 60–61, 70–73, 75, 82–83, 88–91, 92 (left), 95 (right), 96–97, 99 (left), 103 (right), 104 (bottom right), 108 (top left, middle), 112, 118–119, 127

Collage Projects by Sunny Koch:
Pages 6, 8, 26–27, 54, 57 (top), 58, 62–68, 74, 76, 78, 84–85, 87, 92 (right), 94, 95 (left), 98–99 (right), 101, 103 (left), 104 (top and left), 106, 108 (bottom), 109–111, 114–117, 120–122, 124–126

Publications:
Illustration page 67: courtesy *Opportunity Journal Magazine*, 2007
Illustration page 68: courtesy *Guideposts* magazine, 2002
Illustration page 87: courtesy *Hallmark Magazine*, Fall 2004
Invitation page 106: courtesy The National Organization for Hearing Research Foundation
Illustration page 115: courtesy *Guideposts* magazine, 2001

Additional Photography: Thomas Burke pages 26–27, 54, 58, 68, 76, 84–85, 87, 106, 110, 114–116, 122, 124

{ *Acknowledgments* }

We gratefully thank Jennifer Barry, for her exquisite design and concept—a lovely collaboration; Kristen Hall, for her technical and creative assistance; Carolyn Miller, for her wonderful assemblage of words; Wendy Candelaria, for her keen photographic eye and loving support; our copyeditor, Julie Holland, for her close attention to detail; Jonathan Koch, for his timeless creative support and encouragement; Lisa Ford, for her delightful company at flea markets and paper fairs; Laura Belt and Patricia and Stephanie Loftus, for their dear friendship and fabulous treasures and embellishments; Rockport Publishers, for making this book a reality; and our students, family, and friends, for enriching our artistic journey.